PENGUIN BOOKS — GREAT IDEAS

*The Significance of the Frontier
in American History*

Frederick Jackson Turner
1861–1932

Frederick Jackson Turner

The Significance of the Frontier in American History

PENGUIN BOOKS — GREAT IDEAS

PENGUIN BOOKS

Published by the Penguin Group
Penguin Books Ltd, 80 Strand, London WC2R ORL, England
Penguin Group (USA) Inc., 375 Hudson Street, New York, New York 10014, USA
Penguin Group (Canada), 90 Eglinton Avenue East, Suite 700, Toronto, Ontario, Canada M4P 2Y3
(a division of Pearson Penguin Canada Inc.)
Penguin Ireland, 25 St Stephen's Green, Dublin 2, Ireland (a division of Penguin Books Ltd)
Penguin Group (Australia), 250 Camberwell Road, Camberwell, Victoria 3124, Australia
(a division of Pearson Australia Group Pty Ltd)
Penguin Books India Pvt Ltd, 11 Community Centre, Panchsheel Park, New Delhi – 110 017, India
Penguin Group (NZ), 67 Apollo Drive, Rosedale, North Shore 0632, New Zealand
(a division of Pearson New Zealand Ltd)
Penguin Books (South Africa) (Pty) Ltd, 24 Sturdee Avenue, Rosebank, Johannesburg 2196, South Africa

Penguin Books Ltd, Registered Offices: 80 Strand, London WC2R ORL, England

www.penguin.com

The Frontier in American History first published 1920
This selection first published 2008
2

All rights reserved

Set by Rowland Phototypesetting Ltd, Bury St Edmunds, Suffolk
Printed in England by Clays Ltd, St Ives plc

978-0-141-04257-2

www.greenpenguin.co.uk

Penguin Books is committed to a sustainable future
for our business, our readers and our planet.
The book in your hands is made from paper
certified by the Forest Stewardship Council.

Contents

The Significance of the Frontier in American History (1893)

In a recent bulletin of the Superintendent of the Census for 1890 appear these significant words: 'Up to and including 1880 the country had a frontier of settlement, but at present the unsettled area has been so broken into by isolated bodies of settlement that there can hardly be said to be a frontier line. In the discussion of its extent, its westward movement, etc., it can not, therefore, any longer have a place in the census reports.' This brief official statement marks the closing of a great historic movement. Up to our own day American history has been in a large degree the history of the colonization of the Great West. The existence of an area of free land, its continuous recession, and the advance of American settlement westward, explain American development.

Behind institutions, behind constitutional forms and modifications, lie the vital forces that call these organs into life and shape them to meet changing conditions. The peculiarity of American institutions is, the fact that they have been compelled to adapt themselves to the changes of an expanding people – to the changes involved in crossing a continent, in winning a wilderness, and in developing at each area of this progress out of the primitive economic and political conditions of the frontier into the complexity of city life. Said Calhoun in 1817, 'We are great, and rapidly – I was about to say fearfully – growing!' So saying, he touched the distinguishing feature of American life. All peoples show development; the germ theory of politics has been sufficiently emphasized. In the case of most nations, however, the development has occurred in a limited area; and if the nation has expanded, it has met other growing peoples whom it has conquered. But in the case of the United States we have a different phenomenon. Limiting our attention to the Atlantic coast, we have the familiar phenomenon of the evolution of institutions in a limited area, such as the rise of representative government; the differentiation of simple colonial governments into complex organs; the progress from primitive industrial society, without division of labor, up to manufacturing civilization. But we have in addition to this a recurrence of the process of evolution in each western area reached in the process of expansion. Thus American development has exhibited not merely advance along a single line, but a return to primitive conditions on a continually advancing frontier line, and a new development for that area. American social development has been continually beginning over again on the frontier. This perennial rebirth, this fluidity of American life, this expansion westward with its new opportunities, its continuous touch with the simplicity of primitive society, furnish the forces dominating American character. The true point of view in the history of this nation is not the Atlantic coast, it is the Great West. Even the slavery struggle, which is made so exclusive an object of attention by writers like Professor von Holst, occupies its important place in American history because of its relation to westward expansion.

In this advance, the frontier is the outer edge of the wave – the meeting point between savagery and civilization. Much has been written about the frontier from the point of view of border warfare and the chase, but as a field for the serious study of the economist and the historian it has been neglected.

The American frontier is sharply distinguished from the European frontier – a fortified boundary line running through dense populations. The most significant thing about the American frontier is, that it lies at the hither edge of free land. In the census reports it is treated as the margin of that settlement which has a density of two or more to the square mile. The term is an elastic one, and for our purposes does not need sharp definition. We shall consider the whole frontier belt, including the Indian country and the outer margin of the 'settled area' of the census reports. This paper will make no attempt to treat the subject exhaustively; its aim is simply to call attention to the frontier as a fertile field for investigation, and to suggest some of the problems which arise in connection with it.

In the settlement of America we have to observe how European life entered the continent, and how America modified and developed that life and reacted on Europe. Our early history is the study of European germs developing in an American environment. Too exclusive attention has been paid by institutional students to the Germanic origins, too little to the

American factors. The frontier is the line of most rapid and effective Americanization. The wilderness masters the colonist. It finds him a European in dress, industries, tools, modes of travel, and thought. It takes him from the railroad car and puts him in the birch canoe. It strips off the garments of civilization and arrays him in the hunting shirt and the moccasin. It puts him in the log cabin of the Cherokee and Iroquois and runs an Indian palisade around him. Before long he has gone to planting Indian corn and plowing with a sharp stick; he shouts the war cry and takes the scalp in orthodox Indian fashion. In short, at the frontier the environment is at first too strong for the man. He must accept the conditions which it furnishes, or perish, and so he fits himself into the Indian clearings and follows the Indian trails. Little by little he transforms the wilderness, but the outcome is not the old Europe, not simply the development of Germanic germs, any more than the first phenomenon was a case of reversion to the Germanic mark. The fact is, that here is a new product that is American. At first, the frontier was the Atlantic coast. It was the frontier of Europe in a very real sense. Moving westward, the frontier became more and more American. As successive terminal moraines result from successive glaciations, so each frontier leaves its traces behind it, and when it becomes a settled area the region still partakes of the frontier characteristics. Thus the advance of the frontier has meant a steady movement away from the influence of Europe, a steady growth of independence on American lines. And to study this advance, the men who grew up under these conditions, and the political, economic, and social results of it, is to study the really American part of our history.

In the course of the seventeenth century the frontier was advanced up the Atlantic river courses, just beyond the 'fall line,' and the tidewater region became the settled area. In the first half of the eighteenth century another advance occurred. Traders followed the Delaware and Shawnese Indians to the Ohio as early as the end of the first quarter of the century. Gov. Spotswood, of Virginia, made an expedition in 1714 across the Blue Ridge. The end of the first quarter of the century saw the advance of the Scotch-Irish and the Palatine Germans up the Shenandoah Valley into the western part of Virginia, and along the Piedmont region of the Carolinas. The Germans in New York pushed the frontier of settlement up the Mohawk to German Flats. In Pennsylvania the town of Bedford indicates the line of settlement. Settlements soon began on the New River, or the Great Kanawha, and on the sources of the Yadkin and French Broad. The King attempted to arrest the advance by his proclamation of 1763, forbidding settlements beyond the sources of the rivers flowing into the Atlantic; but in vain. In the period of the Revolution the frontier crossed the Alleghanies into Kentucky and Tennessee, and the upper waters of the Ohio were settled. When the first census was taken in 1790, the continuous settled area was bounded by a line which ran near the coast of Maine, and included New England except a portion of Vermont and New Hampshire, New York along the Hudson and up the Mohawk about Schenectady, eastern and southern Pennsylvania, Virginia well across the Shenandoah Valley, and the Carolinas and eastern Georgia. Beyond this region of continuous settlement were the small settled areas of Kentucky and Tennessee, and the Ohio, with the mountains intervening between them and the Atlantic area, thus giving a new and important character to the frontier. The isolation of the region increased its peculiarly American tendencies, and the need of transportation facilities to connect it with the East called out important schemes of internal improvement, which will be noted farther on. The 'West,' as a self-conscious section, began to evolve.

From decade to decade distinct advances of the frontier occurred. By the census of 1820 the settled area included Ohio, southern Indiana and Illinois, southeastern Missouri, and about one-half of Louisiana. This settled area had surrounded Indian areas, and the management of these tribes became an object of political concern. The frontier region of the time lay along the Great Lakes, where Astor's American Fur Company operated in the Indian trade, and beyond the Mississippi, where Indian traders extended their activity even to the Rocky Mountains; Florida also furnished frontier conditions. The Mississippi River region was the scene of typical frontier settlements.

The rising steam navigation on western waters, the opening of the Erie Canal, and the westward extension of cotton culture added five frontier states to the Union in this period. Grund, writing in 1836, declares: 'It appears then that the universal disposition of Americans to emigrate to the western wilderness, in order to enlarge their dominion over inanimate nature, is the actual result of an expansive power which is inherent in them, and which by continually agitating all classes of society is constantly throwing a large portion of the whole population on the extreme confines of the State, in order to gain space for its development. Hardly is a new State or Territory formed before the same principle manifests itself again and gives rise to a further emigration; and so is it destined to go on until a physical barrier must finally obstruct its progress.'

In the middle of this century the line indicated by the present eastern boundary of Indian Territory, Nebraska, and Kansas marked the frontier of the Indian country. Minnesota and Wisconsin still exhibited frontier conditions, but the distinctive frontier of the period is found in California, where the gold discoveries had sent a sudden tide of adventurous miners, and in Oregon, and the settlements in Utah. As the frontier had leaped over the Alleghanies, so now it skipped the Great Plains and the Rocky Mountains; and in the same way that the advance of the frontiersmen beyond the Alleghanies had caused the rise of important questions of transportation and internal improvement, so now the settlers beyond the Rocky Mountains needed means of communication with the East, and in the furnishing of these arose the settlement of the Great Plains and the development of still another kind of frontier life. Railroads, fostered by land grants, sent an increasing tide of immigrants into the Far West. The United States Army fought a series of Indian wars in Minnesota, Dakota, and the Indian Territory.

By 1880 the settled area had been pushed into northern

Michigan, Wisconsin, and Minnesota, along Dakota rivers, and in the Black Hills region, and was ascending the rivers of Kansas and Nebraska. The development of mines in Colorado had drawn isolated frontier settlements into that region, and Montana and Idaho were receiving settlers. The frontier was found in these mining camps and the ranches of the Great Plains. The superintendent of the census for 1890 reports, as previously stated, that the settlements of the West lie so scattered over the region that there can no longer be said to be a frontier line.

In these successive frontiers we find natural boundary lines which have served to mark and to affect the characteristics of the frontiers, namely: the 'fall line;' the Alleghany Mountains; the Mississippi; the Missouri where its direction approximates north and south; the line of the arid lands, approximately the ninety-ninth meridian; and the Rocky Mountains. The fall line marked the frontier of the seventeenth century; the Alleghanies that of the eighteenth; the Mississippi that of the first quarter of the nineteenth; the Missouri that of the middle of this century (omitting the California movement); and the belt of the Rocky Mountains and the arid tract, the present frontier. Each was won by a series of Indian wars.

At the Atlantic frontier one can study the germs of processes repeated at each successive frontier. We have the complex European life sharply precipitated by the wilderness into the simplicity of primitive conditions. The first frontier had to meet its Indian question, its question of the disposition of the public domain, of the means of intercourse with older settlements, of the extension of political organization, of religious and educational activity. And the settlement of these and similar questions for one frontier served as a guide for the next. The American student needs not to go to the 'prim little townships of Sleswick' for illustrations of the law of continuity and development. For example, he may study the origin of our land policies in the colonial land policy; he may see how the system grew by adapting the statutes to the customs of the successive frontiers. He may see how the mining experience in the lead regions of Wisconsin, Illinois, and Iowa was applied to the mining laws of the Sierras, and how our Indian policy has been a series of experimentations on successive frontiers. Each tier of new States has found in the older ones material for its constitutions. Each frontier has made similar contributions to American character, as will be discussed farther on.

But with all these similarities there are essential differences, due to the place element and the time element. It is evident that the farming frontier of the Mississippi Valley presents different conditions from the mining frontier of the Rocky Mountains. The frontier reached by the Pacific Railroad, surveyed into rectangles, guarded by the United States Army, and recruited by the daily immigrant ship, moves forward at a swifter pace and in a different way than the frontier reached by the birch canoe or the pack horse. The geologist traces patiently the shores of ancient seas, maps their areas, and compares the older and the newer. It would be a work worth the historian's labors to mark these various frontiers and in detail compare one with another. Not only would there result a more adequate conception of American development and characteristics, but invaluable additions would be made to the history of society.

Loria, the Italian economist, has urged the study of colonial life as an aid in understanding the stages of European development, affirming that colonial settlement is for economic science what the mountain is for geology, bringing to light primitive stratifications. 'America,' he says, 'has the key to the historical enigma which Europe has sought for centuries in vain, and the land which has no history reveals luminously the course of universal history.' There is much truth in this. The United States lies like a huge page in the history of society. Line by line as we read this continental page from West to East we find the record of social evolution. It begins with the Indian and the hunter; it goes on to tell of the disintegration of savagery by the entrance of the trader, the pathfinder of civilization; we read the annals of the pastoral stage in ranch life; the exploitation of the soil by the raising of unrotated crops of corn and wheat in sparsely settled farming communities; the intensive culture of the denser farm settlement; and finally the manufacturing organization with city and factory system. This page is familiar to the student of census statistics, but how little of it has been used by our historians. Particularly in eastern States this page is a palimpsest. What is now a manufacturing State was in an earlier decade an area of intensive farming. Earlier yet it had been a wheat area, and still earlier the 'range' had attracted the cattle-herder. Thus Wisconsin, now developing manufacture, is a State with varied agricultural interests. But earlier it was given over to almost exclusive grain-raising, like North Dakota at the present time.

Each of these areas has had an influence in our economic and political history; the evolution of each into a higher stage has worked political transformations. But what constitutional historian has made any adequate attempt to interpret political facts by the light of these social areas and changes?

The Atlantic frontier was compounded of fisherman, fur-trader, miner, cattle-raiser, and farmer. Excepting the fisherman, each type of industry was on the march toward the West, impelled by an irresistible attraction. Each passed in successive waves across the continent. Stand at Cumberland Gap and watch the procession of civilization, marching single file – the buffalo following the trail to the salt springs, the Indian, the fur-trader and hunter, the cattle-raiser, the pioneer farmer – and the frontier has passed by. Stand at South Pass in the Rockies a century later and see the same procession with wider intervals between. The unequal rate of advance compels us to distinguish the frontier into the trader's frontier, the rancher's frontier, or the miner's frontier, and the farmer's frontier. When the mines and the cowpens were still near the fall line the traders' pack trains were tinkling across the Alleghanies, and the French on the Great Lakes were fortifying their posts, alarmed by the British trader's birch canoe. When the trappers scaled the Rockies, the farmer was still near the mouth of the Missouri.

Why was it that the Indian trader passed so rapidly

across the continent? What effects followed from the trader's frontier? The trade was coeval with American discovery. The Norsemen, Vespuccius, Verrazani, Hudson, John Smith, all trafficked for furs. The Plymouth pilgrims settled in Indian cornfields, and their first return cargo was of beaver and lumber. The records of the various New England colonies show how steadily exploration was carried into the wilderness by this trade. What is true for New England is, as would be expected, even plainer for the rest of the colonies. All along the coast from Maine to Georgia the Indian trade opened up the river courses. Steadily the trader passed westward, utilizing the older lines of French trade. The Ohio, the Great Lakes, the Mississippi, the Missouri, and the Platte, the lines of western advance, were ascended by traders. They found the passes in the Rocky Mountains and guided Lewis and Clark, Frémont, and Bidwell. The explanation of the rapidity of this advance is connected with the effects of the trader on the Indian. The trading post left the unarmed tribes at the mercy of those that had purchased fire-arms – a truth which the Iroquois Indians wrote in blood, and so the remote and unvisited tribes gave eager welcome to the trader. 'The savages,' wrote La Salle, 'take better care of us French than of their own children; from us only can they get guns and goods.' This accounts for the trader's power and the rapidity of his advance. Thus the disintegrating forces of civilization entered the wilderness. Every river valley and Indian trail became a fissure in Indian society, and so that society became honeycombed. Long before the pioneer farmer appeared on the scene, primitive Indian life had passed away. The farmers met Indians armed with guns. The trading frontier, while steadily undermining Indian power by making the tribes ultimately dependent on the whites, yet, through its sale of guns, gave to the Indian increased power of resistance to the farming frontier. French colonization was dominated by its trading frontier; English colonization by its farming frontier. There was an antagonism between the two frontiers as between the two nations. Said Duquesne to the Iroquois, 'Are you ignorant of the difference between the king of England and the king of France? Go see the forts that our king has established and you will see that you can still hunt under their very walls. They have been placed for your advantage in places which you frequent. The English, on the contrary, are no sooner in possession of a place than the game is driven away. The forest falls before them as they advance, and the soil is laid bare so that you can scarce find the wherewithal to erect a shelter for the night.'

And yet, in spite of this opposition of the interests of the trader and the farmer, the Indian trade pioneered the way for civilization. The buffalo trail became the Indian trail, and this became the trader's 'trace;' the trails widened into roads, and the roads into turnpikes, and these in turn were transformed into railroads. The same origin can be shown for the railroads of the South, the Far West, and the Dominion of Canada. The trading posts reached by these trails were on the sites of Indian villages which had been placed in positions suggested by nature; and these trading posts, situated so as to command the water systems of the country, have grown into such cities as Albany, Pittsburgh, Detroit, Chicago, St Louis, Council Bluffs, and Kansas City. Thus civilization in America has followed the arteries made by geology, pouring an ever richer tide through them, until at last the slender paths of aboriginal intercourse have been broadened and interwoven into the complex mazes of modern commercial lines; the wilderness has been interpenetrated by lines of civilization growing ever more numerous. It is like the steady growth of a complex nervous system for the originally simple, inert continent. If one would understand why we are to-day one nation, rather than a collection of isolated states, he must study this economic and social consolidation of the country. In this progress from savage conditions lie topics for the evolutionist.

The effect of the Indian frontier as a consolidating agent in our history is important. From the close of the seventeenth century various intercolonial congresses have been called to treat with Indians and establish common measures of defense. Particularism was strongest in colonies with no Indian frontier. This frontier stretched along the western border like a cord of union. The Indian was a common danger, demanding united action. Most celebrated of these conferences was the Albany congress of 1754, called to treat with the Six Nations, and to consider plans of union. Even a cursory reading of the plan proposed by the congress reveals the importance of the frontier. The powers of the general council and the officers were, chiefly, the determination of peace and war with the Indians, the regulation of Indian trade, the purchase of Indian lands, and the creation and government of new settlements as a security against the Indians. It is evident that the unifying tendencies of the Revolutionary period were facilitated by the previous cooperation in the regulation of the frontier. In this connection may be mentioned the importance of the frontier, from that day to this, as a military training school, keeping alive the power of resistance to aggression, and developing the stalwart and rugged qualities of the frontiersman.

It would not be possible in the limits of this paper to trace the other frontiers across the continent. Travelers of the eighteenth century found the 'cowpens' among the cane-brakes and peavine pastures of the South, and the 'cow drivers' took their droves to Charleston, Philadelphia, and New York. Travelers at the close of the War of 1812 met droves of more than a thousand cattle and swine from the interior of Ohio going to Pennsylvania to fatten for the Philadelphia market. The ranges of the Great Plains, with ranch and cowboy and nomadic life, are things of yesterday and of to-day. The experience of the Carolina cowpens guided the ranchers of Texas. One element favoring the rapid extension of the rancher's frontier is the fact that in a remote country lacking transportation facilities the product must be in small bulk, or must be able to transport itself, and the cattle raiser could easily drive his product to market. The effect of these great ranches on the subsequent agrarian history of the localities in which they existed should be studied.

The maps of the census reports show an uneven advance of the farmer's frontier, with tongues of settlement pushed forward and with indentations of wilderness. In part this is due to Indian resistance, in part to the location of river valleys and passes, in part to the unequal force of the centers of frontier attraction. Among the important centers of attraction may be mentioned the following: fertile and favorably situated soils, salt springs, mines, and army posts.

The frontier army post, serving to protect the settlers from the Indians, has also acted as a wedge to open the Indian country, and has been a nucleus for settlement. In this connection mention should also be made of the government military and exploring expeditions in determining the lines of settlement. But all the more important expeditions were greatly indebted to the earliest pathmakers, the Indian guides, the traders and trappers, and the French voyageurs, who were inevitable parts of governmental expeditions from the days of Lewis and Clark. Each expedition was an epitome of the previous factors in western advance.

In an interesting monograph, Victor Hehn has traced the effect of salt upon early European development, and has pointed out how it affected the lines of settlement and the form of administration. A similar study might be made for the salt springs of the United States. The early settlers were tied to the coast by the need of salt, without which they could not preserve their meats or live in comfort. Writing in 1752, Bishop Spangenburg says of a colony for which he was seeking lands in North Carolina, 'They will require salt & other necessaries which they can neither manufacture nor raise. Either they must go to Charleston, which is 300 miles distant

. . . Or else they must go to Boling's Point in V^a on a branch of the James & is also 300 miles from here . . . Or else they must go down the Roanoke – I know not how many miles – where salt is brought up from the Cape Fear.' This may serve as a typical illustration. An annual pilgrimage to the coast for salt thus became essential. Taking flocks or furs and ginseng root, the early settlers sent their pack trains after seeding time each year to the coast. This proved to be an important educational influence, since it was almost the only way in which the pioneer learned what was going on in the East. But when discovery was made of the salt springs of the Kanawha, and the Holston, and Kentucky, and central New York, the West began to be freed from dependence on the coast. It was in part the effect of finding these salt springs that enabled settlement to cross the mountains.

From the time the mountains rose between the pioneer and the seaboard, a new order of Americanism arose. The West and the East began to get out of touch of each other. The settlements from the sea to the mountains kept connection with the rear and had a certain solidarity. But the over-mountain men grew more and more independent. The East took a narrow view of American advance, and nearly lost these men. Kentucky and Tennessee history bears abundant witness to the truth of this statement. The East began to try to hedge and limit westward expansion. Though Webster could declare that there were no Alleghanies in his politics, yet in politics in general they were a very solid factor.

The exploitation of the beasts took hunter and trader

to the west, the exploitation of the grasses took the rancher west, and the exploitation of the virgin soil of the river valleys and prairies attracted the farmer. Good soils have been the most continuous attraction to the farmer's frontier. The land hunger of the Virginians drew them down the rivers into Carolina, in early colonial days; the search for soils took the Massachusetts men to Pennsylvania and to New York. As the eastern lands were taken up migration flowed across them to the west. Daniel Boone, the great backwoodsman, who combined the occupations of hunter, trader, cattle-raiser, farmer, and surveyor – learning, probably from the traders, of the fertility of the lands of the upper Yadkin, where the traders were wont to rest as they took their way to the Indians, left his Pennsylvania home with his father, and passed down the Great Valley road to that stream. Learning from a trader of the game and rich pastures of Kentucky, he pioneered the way for the farmers to that region. Thence he passed to the frontier of Missouri, where his settlement was long a landmark on the frontier. Here again he helped to open the way for civilization, finding salt licks, and trails, and land. His son was among the earliest trappers in the passes of the Rocky Mountains, and his party are said to have been the first to camp on the present site of Denver. His grandson, Col. A. J. Boone, of Colorado, was a power among the Indians of the Rocky Mountains, and was appointed an agent by the government. Kit Carson's mother was a Boone. Thus this family epitomizes the backwoodsman's advance across the continent.

The farmer's advance came in a distinct series of

waves. In Peck's New Guide to the West, published in Boston in 1837, occurs this suggestive passage:

Generally, in all the western settlements, three classes, like the waves of the ocean, have rolled one after the other. First comes the pioneer, who depends for the subsistence of his family chiefly upon the natural growth of vegetation, called the 'range,' and the proceeds of hunting. His implements of agriculture are rude, chiefly of his own make, and his efforts directed mainly to a crop of corn and a 'truck patch.' The last is a rude garden for growing cabbage, beans, corn for roasting ears, cucumbers, and potatoes. A log cabin, and, occasionally, a stable and corn-crib, and a field of a dozen acres, the timber girdled or 'deadened,' and fenced, are enough for his occupancy. It is quite immaterial whether he ever becomes the owner of the soil. He is the occupant for the time being, pays no rent, and feels as independent as the 'lord of the manor.' With a horse, cow, and one or two breeders of swine, he strikes into the woods with his family, and becomes the founder of a new county, or perhaps state. He builds his cabin, gathers around him a few other families of similar tastes and habits, and occupies till the range is somewhat subdued, and hunting a little precarious, or, which is more frequently the case, till the neighbors crowd around, roads, bridges, and fields annoy him, and he lacks elbow room. The pre-emption law enables him to dispose of his cabin and cornfield to the next class of emigrants; and, to employ his own figures, he 'breaks for the high timber,' 'clears out for the New Purchase,' or migrates to Arkansas or Texas, to work the same process over.

The next class of emigrants purchase the lands, add field

to field, clear out the roads, throw rough bridges over the streams, put up hewn log houses with glass windows and brick or stone chimneys, occasionally plant orchards, build mills, school-houses, court-houses, etc., and exhibit the picture and forms of plain, frugal, civilized life.

Another wave rolls on. The men of capital and enterprise come. The settler is ready to sell out and take the advantage of the rise in property, push farther into the interior and become, himself, a man of capital and enterprise in turn. The small village rises to a spacious town or city; substantial edifices of brick, extensive fields, orchards, gardens, colleges, and churches are seen. Broadcloths, silks, leghorns, crapes, and all the refinements, luxuries, elegancies, frivolities, and fashions are in vogue. Thus wave after wave is rolling westward; the real Eldorado is still farther on.

A portion of the two first classes remain stationary amidst the general movement, improve their habits and condition, and rise in the scale of society.

The writer has traveled much amongst the first class, the real pioneers. He has lived many years in connection with the second grade; and now the third wave is sweeping over large districts of Indiana, Illinois, and Missouri. Migration has become almost a habit in the West. Hundreds of men can be found, not over 50 years of age, who have settled for the fourth, fifth, or sixth time on a new spot. To sell out and remove only a few hundred miles makes up a portion of the variety of backwoods life and manners.

Omitting those of the pioneer farmers who move from the love of adventure, the advance of the more steady farmer is easy to understand. Obviously the immigrant was attracted by the cheap lands of the frontier, and even the native farmer felt their influence strongly. Year by year the farmers who lived on soil whose returns were diminished by unrotated crops were offered the virgin soil of the frontier at nominal prices. Their growing families demanded more lands, and these were dear. The competition of the unexhausted, cheap, and easily tilled prairie lands compelled the farmer either to go west and continue the exhaustion of the soil on a new frontier, or to adopt intensive culture. Thus the census of 1890 shows, in the Northwest, many counties in which there is an absolute or a relative decrease of population. These States have been sending farmers to advance the frontier on the plains, and have themselves begun to turn to intensive farming and to manufacture. A decade before this, Ohio had shown the same transition stage. Thus the demand for land and the love of wilderness freedom drew the frontier ever onward.

Having now roughly outlined the various kinds of frontiers, and their modes of advance, chiefly from the point of view of the frontier itself, we may next inquire what were the influences on the East and on the Old World. A rapid enumeration of some of the more noteworthy effects is all that I have time for.

First, we note that the frontier promoted the formation of a composite nationality for the American people. The coast was preponderantly English, but the later tides of continental immigration flowed across to the free lands. This was the case from the early colonial days. The Scotch-Irish and the Palatine Germans, or 'Pennsylvania Dutch,' furnished the dominant element in the stock of the colonial frontier. With these peoples were also the freed indented servants, or redemptioners, who at the expiration of their time of service passed to the frontier. Governor Spotswood of Virginia writes in 1717, 'The inhabitants of our frontiers are composed generally of such as have been transported hither as servants, and, being out of their time, settle themselves where land is to be taken up and that will produce the necessarys of life with little labour.' Very generally these re-demptioners were of non-English stock. In the crucible of the frontier the immigrants were Americanized, liber-ated, and fused into a mixed race, English in neither nationality nor characteristics. The process has gone on from the early days to our own. Burke and other writers in the middle of the eighteenth century believed that Pennsylvania was 'threatened with the danger of being wholly foreign in language, manners, and perhaps even inclinations.' The German and Scotch-Irish elements in the frontier of the South were only less great. In the middle of the present century the German element in Wisconsin was already so considerable that leading pub-licists looked to the creation of a German state out of the commonwealth by concentrating their colonization. Such examples teach us to beware of misinterpreting the fact that there is a common English speech in America into a belief that the stock is also English.

In another way the advance of the frontier decreased our dependence on England. The coast, particularly of the South, lacked diversified industries, and was depen-dent on England for the bulk of its supplies. In the South there was even a dependence on the Northern colonies for articles of food. Governor Glenn, of South Carolina, writes in the middle of the eighteenth century: 'Our trade with New York and Philadelphia was of this sort, draining us of all the little money and bills we could gather from other places for their bread, flour, beer, hams, bacon, and other things of their produce, all which, except beer, our new townships begin to supply us with, which are settled with very industrious and thriving Germans. This no doubt diminishes the number of shipping and the appearance of our trade, but it is far from being a detriment to us.' Before long the frontier created a demand for merchants. As it retreated from the coast it became less and less possible for England to bring her supplies directly to the consumer's wharfs, and carry away staple crops, and staple crops began to give way to diversified agriculture for a time. The effect of this phase of the frontier action upon the northern section is perceived when we realize how the advance of the frontier aroused seaboard cities like Boston, New York, and Baltimore, to engage in rivalry for what Washington called 'the extensive and valuable trade of a rising empire.'

The legislation which most developed the powers of the national government, and played the largest part in its activity, was conditioned on the frontier. Writers have discussed the subjects of tariff, land, and internal improvement, as subsidiary to the slavery question. But when American history comes to be rightly viewed it will be seen that the slavery question is an incident. In the period from the end of the first half of the present century to the close of the Civil War slavery rose to primary, but far from exclusive, importance. But this does not justify Dr von Holst (to take an example) in treating our constitutional history in its formative period down to 1828 in a single volume, giving six volumes chiefly to the history of slavery from 1828 to 1861, under the title 'Constitutional History of the United States.' The growth of nationalism and the evolution of American political institutions were dependent on the advance of the frontier. Even so recent a writer as Rhodes, in his 'History of the United States since the Compromise of 1850,' has treated the legislation called out by the western advance as incidental to the slavery struggle.

This is a wrong perspective. The pioneer needed the goods of the coast, and so the grand series of internal improvement and railroad legislation began, with potent nationalizing effects. Over internal improvements occurred great debates, in which grave constitutional questions were discussed. Sectional groupings appear in the votes, profoundly significant for the historian. Loose construction increased as the nation marched westward. But the West was not content with bringing the farm to the factory. Under the lead of Clay – 'Harry of the West' – protective tariffs were passed, with the cry of bringing the factory to the farm. The disposition of the public lands was a third important subject of national legislation influenced by the frontier.

The public domain has been a force of profound importance in the nationalization and development of the government. The effects of the struggle of the landed and the landless States, and of the Ordinance of 1787, need no discussion. Administratively the frontier called out some of the highest and most vitalizing activities of the general government. The purchase of Louisiana was perhaps the constitutional turning point in the history of the Republic, inasmuch as it afforded both a new area for national legislation and the occasion of the downfall of the policy of strict construction. But the purchase of Louisiana was called out by frontier needs and demands. As frontier States accrued to the Union the national power grew. In a speech on the dedication of the Calhoun monument Mr Lamar explained: 'In 1789 the States were the creators of the Federal Government; in 1861 the Federal Government was the creator of a large majority of the States.'

When we consider the public domain from the point of view of the sale and disposal of the public lands we are again brought face to face with the frontier. The policy of the United States in dealing with its lands is in sharp contrast with the European system of scientific administration. Efforts to make this domain a source of revenue, and to withhold it from emigrants in order that settlement might be compact, were in vain. The jealousy and the fears of the East were powerless in the face of the demands of the frontiersmen. John Quincy Adams was obliged to confess: 'My own system of administration, which was to make the national domain the inexhaustible fund for progressive and unceasing internal improvement, has failed.' The reason is obvious; a system of administration was not what the West demanded; it wanted land. Adams states the situation as follows: 'The slaveholders of the South have bought the co-operation of the western country by the bribe of the western lands, abandoning to the new Western States their own proportion of the public property and aiding them in the design of grasping all the lands into their own hands. Thomas H. Benton was the author of this system, which he brought forward as a substitute for the American system of Mr Clay, and to supplant him as the leading statesman of the West. Mr Clay, by his tariff compromise with Mr Calhoun, abandoned his own American system. At the same time he brought forward a plan for distributing among all the States of the Union the proceeds of the sales of the public lands. His bill for that purpose passed both House of Congress, but was vetoed by President Jackson, who, in his annual message of December, 1832, formally recommended that all public lands should be gratuitously given away to individual adventurers and to the States in which the lands are situated.'

'No subject,' said Henry Clay, 'which has presented itself to the present, or perhaps any preceding, Congress, is of greater magnitude than that of the public lands.' When we consider the far-reaching effects of the government's land policy upon political, economic, and social aspects of American life, we are disposed to agree with him. But this legislation was framed under frontier influences, and under the lead of Western statesmen like Benton and Jackson. Said Senator Scott of Indiana in 1841: 'I consider the pre-emption law merely declaratory of the custom or common law of the settlers.'

It is safe to say that the legislation with regard to land, tariff, and internal improvements – the American system of the nationalizing Whig party – was conditioned on frontier ideas and needs. But it was not merely in legislative action that the frontier worked against the sectionalism of the coast. The economic and social characteristics of the frontier worked against sectionalism. The men of the frontier had closer resemblances to the Middle region than to either of the other sections. Pennsylvania had been the seed-plot of frontier emigration, and, although she passed on her settlers along the Great Valley into the west of Virginia and the Carolinas, yet the industrial society of these Southern frontiersmen was always more like that of the Middle region than like that of the tide-water portion of the South, which later came to spread its industrial type throughout the South.

The Middle region, entered by New York harbor, was an open door to all Europe. The tide-water part of the South represented typical Englishmen, modified by a warm climate and servile labor, and living in baronial fashion on great plantations; New England stood for a special English movement – Puritanism. The Middle region was less English than the other sections. It had a wide mixture of nationalities, a varied society, the mixed town and county system of local government, a varied economic life, many religious sects. In short, it was a region mediating between New England and the South, and the East and the West. It represented that composite nationality which the contemporary United States exhibits, that juxtaposition of non-English groups, occupying a valley or a little settlement, and presenting reflections of the map of Europe in their variety. It was democratic and nonsectional, if not national; 'easy, tolerant, and contented;' rooted strongly in material prosperity. It was typical of the modern United States. It was least sectional, not only because it lay between North and South, but also because with no barriers to shut out its frontiers from its settled region, and with a system of connecting waterways, the Middle region mediated between East and West as well as between North and South. Thus it became the typically American region. Even the New Englander, who was shut out from the frontier by the Middle region, tarrying in New York or Pennsylvania on his westward march, lost the acuteness of his sectionalism on the way.

The spread of cotton culture into the interior of the South finally broke down the contrast between the 'tide-water' region and the rest of the State, and based Southern interests on slavery. Before this process revealed its results the western portion of the South, which was akin to Pennsylvania in stock, society, and industry, showed tendencies to fall away from the faith of the fathers into internal improvement legislation and nationalism. In the Virginia convention of 1829–30, called to revise the constitution, Mr Leigh, of Chesterfield, one of the tide-water counties, declared:

One of the main causes of discontent which led to this convention, that which had the strongest influence in overcoming our veneration for the work of our fathers, which taught us to contemn the sentiments of Henry and Mason and Pendleton, which weaned us from our reverence for the constituted authorities of the State, was an overweening passion for internal improvement. I say this with perfect knowledge, for it has been avowed to me by gentlemen from the West over and over again. And let me tell the gentleman from Albemarle (Mr Gordon) that it has been another principal object of those who set this ball of revolution in motion, to overturn the doctrine of State rights, of which Virginia has been the very pillar, and to remove the barrier she has interposed to the interference of the Federal Government in that same work of internal improvement, by so reorganizing the legislature that Virginia, too, may be hitched to the Federal car.

It was this nationalizing tendency of the West that transformed the democracy of Jefferson into the national republicanism of Monroe and the democracy of Andrew Jackson. The West of the War of 1812, the West of Clay, and Benton and Harrison, and Andrew Jackson, shut off by the Middle States and the mountains from the coast sections, had a solidarity of its own with national tendencies. On the tide of the Father of Waters, North and South met and mingled into a nation. Interstate migration went steadily on – a process of cross-fertilization of ideas and institutions. The fierce struggle of the sections over slavery on the western frontier does not diminish the truth of this statement; it proves the truth of it. Slavery was a sectional trait that would not lie down, but in the West it could not remain sectional. It was the greatest of frontiersmen who declared: 'I believe this Government can not endure permanently half slave and half free. It will become all of one thing or all of the other.'

Nothing works for nationalism like intercourse within the nation. Mobility of population is death to localism, and the western frontier worked irresistibly in unsettling population. The effect reached back from the frontier and affected profoundly the Atlantic coast and even the Old World.

But the most important effect of the frontier has been in the promotion of democracy here and in Europe. As has been indicated, the frontier is productive of individualism. Complex society is precipitated by the wilderness into a kind of primitive organization based on the family. The tendency is anti-social. It produces antipathy to control, and particularly to any direct control. The tax-gatherer is viewed as a representative of oppression. Prof. Osgood, in an able article, has pointed out that the frontier conditions prevalent in the colonies are important factors in the explanation of the American Revolution, where individual liberty was sometimes confused with absence of all effective government. The same conditions aid in explaining the difficulty of instituting a strong government in the period of the confederacy. The frontier individualism has from the beginning promoted democracy.

The frontier States that came into the Union in the first quarter of a century of its existence came in with democratic suffrage provisions, and had reactive effects of the highest importance upon the older States whose peoples were being attracted there. An extension of the franchise became essential. It was *western* New York that forced an extension of suffrage in the constitutional convention of that State in 1821; and it was *western*

Virginia that compelled the tide-water region to put a more liberal suffrage provision in the constitution framed in 1830, and to give to the frontier region a more nearly proportionate representation with the tide-water aristocracy. The rise of democracy as an effective force in the nation came in with western preponderance under Jackson and William Henry Harrison, and it meant the triumph of the frontier – with all of its good and with all of its evil elements. An interesting illustration of the tone of frontier democracy in 1830 comes from the same debates in the Virginia convention already referred to. A representative from western Virginia declared:

But, sir, it is not the increase of population in the West which this gentleman ought to fear. It is the energy which the mountain breeze and western habits impart to those emigrants. They are regenerated, politically I mean, sir. They soon become *working politicians;* and the difference, sir, between a *talking* and a *working* politician is immense. The Old Dominion has long been celebrated for producing great orators; the ablest metaphysicians in policy; men that can split hairs in all abstruse questions of political economy. But at home, or when they return from Congress, they have negroes to fan them asleep. But a Pennsylvania, a New York, an Ohio, or a western Virginia statesman, though far inferior in logic, metaphysics, and rhetoric to an old Virginia statesman, has this advantage, that when he returns home he takes off his coat and takes hold of the plow. This gives him bone and muscle, sir, and preserves his republican principles pure and uncontaminated.

So long as free land exists, the opportunity for a competency exists, and economic power secures political power. But the democracy born of free land, strong in selfishness and individualism, intolerant of administrative experience and education, and pressing individual liberty beyond its proper bounds, has its dangers as well as its benefits. Individualism in America has allowed a laxity in regard to governmental affairs which has rendered possible the spoils system and all the manifest evils that follow from the lack of a highly developed civic spirit. In this connection may be noted also the influence of frontier conditions in permitting lax business honor, inflated paper currency and wild-cat banking. The colonial and revolutionary frontier was the region whence emanated many of the worst forms of an evil currency. The West in the War of 1812 repeated the phenomenon on the frontier of that day, while the speculation and wild-cat banking of the period of the crisis of 1837 occurred on the new frontier belt of the next tier of States. Thus each one of the periods of lax financial integrity coincides with periods when a new set of frontier communities had arisen, and coincides in area with these successive frontiers, for the most part. The recent Populist agitation is a case in point. Many a State that now declines any connection with the tenets of the Populists, itself adhered to such ideas in an earlier stage of the development of the State. A primitive society can hardly be expected to show the intelligent appreciation of the complexity of business interests in a developed society. The continual recurrence of these areas of paper-money agitation is another evidence that the frontier can be isolated and studied as a factor in American history of the highest importance.[1]

The East has always feared the result of an unregulated advance of the frontier, and has tried to check and guide it. The English authorities would have checked settlement at the headwaters of the Atlantic tributaries and allowed the 'savages to enjoy their deserts in quiet lest the peltry trade should decrease.' This called out Burke's splendid protest:

If you stopped your grants, what would be the consequence? The people would occupy without grants. They have already so occupied in many places. You can not station garrisons in every part of these deserts. If you drive the people from one place, they will carry on their annual tillage and remove with their flocks and herds to another. Many of the people in the back settlements are already little attached to particular situations. Already they have topped the Appalachian Mountains. From thence they behold before them an immense plain, one vast, rich, level meadow; a square of five hundred miles. Over this they would wander without a possibility of restraint; they would change their manners with their habits of life;

---

[1] I have refrained from dwelling on the lawless characteristics of the frontier, because they are sufficiently well known. The gambler and desperado, the regulators of the Carolinas and the vigilantes of California, are types of that line of scum that the waves of advancing civilization bore before them, and of the growth of spontaneous organs of authority where legal authority was absent. The humor, bravery, and rude strength, as well as the vices of the frontier in its worst aspect, have left traces on American character, language, and literature, not soon to be effaced.

would soon forget a government by which they were disowned; would become hordes of English Tartars; and, pouring down upon your unfortified frontiers a fierce and irresistible cavalry, become masters of your governors and your counselers, your collectors and comptrollers, and of all the slaves that adhered to them. Such would, and in no long time must, be the effect of attempting to forbid as a crime and to suppress as an evil the command and blessing of Providence, 'Increase and multiply.' Such would be the happy result of an endeavor to keep as a lair of wild beasts that earth which God, by an express charter, has given to the children of men.

But the English Government was not alone in its desire to limit the advance of the frontier and guide its destinies. Tidewater Virginia and South Carolina gerrymandered those colonies to insure the dominance of the coast in their legislatures. Washington desired to settle a State at a time in the Northwest; Jefferson would reserve from settlement the territory of his Louisiana Purchase north of the thirty-second parallel, in order to offer it to the Indians in exchange for their settlements east of the Mississippi. 'When we shall be full on this side,' he writes, 'we may lay off a range of States on the western bank from the head to the mouth, and so range after range, advancing compactly as we multiply.' Madison went so far as to argue to the French minister that the United States had no interest in seeing population extend itself on the right bank of the Mississippi, but should rather fear it. When the Oregon question was under debate, in 1824, Smyth, of Virginia, would draw an unchangeable line for the limits of the United States at the outer limit of two tiers of States beyond the Mississippi, complaining that the seaboard States were being drained of the flower of their population by the bringing of too much land into market. Even Thomas Benton, the man of widest views of the destiny of the West, at this stage of his career declared that along the ridge of the Rocky Mountains 'the western limits of the Republic should be drawn, and the statue of the fabled god Terminus should be raised upon its highest peak, never to be thrown down.' But the attempts to limit the boundaries, to restrict land sales and settlement, and to deprive the West of its share of political power were all in vain. Steadily the frontier of settlement advanced and carried with it individualism, democracy, and nationalism, and powerfully affected the East and the Old World.

The most effective efforts of the East to regulate the frontier came through its educational and religious activity, exerted by interstate migration and by organized societies. Speaking in 1835, Dr Lyman Beecher declared: 'It is equally plain that the religious and political destiny of our nation is to be decided in the West,' and he pointed out that the population of the West 'is assembled from all the States of the Union and from all the nations of Europe, and is rushing in like the water of the flood, demanding for its moral preservation the immediate and universal action of those institutions which discipline the mind and arm the conscience and the heart. And so various are the opinions and habits, and so recent and imperfect is the acquaintance, and so sparse are the settlements of the West, that no homogeneous public sentiment can be formed to legislate immediately into being the requisite institutions. And yet they are all needed immediately in their utmost perfection and power. A nation is being "born in a day." . . . But what will become of the West if her prosperity rushes up to such a majesty of power, while those great institutions linger which are necessary to form the mind and the conscience and the heart of that vast world. It must not be permitted . . . Let no man at the East quiet himself and dream of liberty, whatever may become of the West . . . Her destiny is our destiny.'

With the appeal to the conscience of New England, he adds appeals to her fears lest other religious sects anticipate her own. The New England preacher and school-teacher left their mark on the West. The dread of Western emancipation from New England's political and economic control was paralleled by her fears lest the West cut loose from her religion. Commenting in 1850 on reports that settlement was rapidly extending northward in Wisconsin, the editor of the *Home Missionary* writes: 'We scarcely know whether to rejoice or mourn over this extension of our settlements. While we sympathize in whatever tends to increase the physical resources and prosperity of our country, we can not forget that with all these dispersions into remote and still remoter corners of the land the supply of the means of grace is becoming relatively less and less.' Acting in accordance with such ideas, home missions were established and Western colleges were erected. As seaboard cities like Philadelphia, New York, and Baltimore strove for the mastery of Western trade, so the various denominations strove for the possession of the West. Thus an intellectual stream from New England sources fertilized the West. Other sections sent their missionaries; but the real struggle was between sects. The contest for power and the expansive tendency furnished to the various sects by the existence of a moving frontier must have had important results on the character of religious organization in the United States. The multiplication of rival churches in the little frontier towns had deep and lasting social effects. The religious aspects of the frontier make a chapter in our history which needs study.

From the conditions of frontier life came intellectual traits of profound importance. The works of travelers along each frontier from colonial days onward describe certain common traits, and these traits have, while softening down, still persisted as survivals in the place of their origin, even when a higher social organization succeeded. The result is that to the frontier the American intellect owes its striking characteristics. That coarseness and strength combined with acuteness and inquisitiveness; that practical, inventive turn of mind, quick to find expedients; that masterful grasp of material things, lacking in the artistic but powerful to effect great ends; that restless, nervous energy; that dominant individualism, working for good and for evil, and withal that buoyancy and exuberance which comes with freedom – these are traits of the frontier, or traits called out elsewhere because of the existence of the frontier. Since the days when the fleet of Columbus sailed into the waters of the New World, America has been another name for opportunity, and the people of the United States have taken their tone from the incessant expansion which has not only been open but has even been forced upon them. He would be a rash prophet who should assert that the expansive character of American life has now entirely ceased. Movement has been its dominant fact, and, unless this training has no effect upon a people, the American energy will continually demand a wider field for its exercise. But never again will such gifts of free land offer themselves. For a moment, at the frontier, the bonds of custom are broken and unrestraint is triumphant. There is not *tabula rasa*. The stubborn American environment is there with its imperious summons to accept its conditions; the inherited ways of doing things are also there; and yet, in spite of environment, and in spite of custom, each frontier did indeed furnish a new field of opportunity, a gate of escape from the bondage of the past; and freshness, and confidence, and scorn of older society, impatience of its restraints and its ideas, and indifference to its lessons, have accompanied the frontier. What the Mediterranean Sea was to the Greeks, breaking the bond of custom, offering new experiences, calling out new institutions and activities, that, and more, the ever retreating frontier has been to the United States directly, and to the nations of Europe more remotely. And now, four centuries from the discovery of America, at the end of a hundred years of life under the Constitution, the frontier has gone, and with its going has closed the first period of American history.

II

The Problem of the West (1896)

The problem of the West is nothing less than the problem of American development. A glance at the map of the United States reveals the truth. To write of a 'Western sectionalism,' bounded on the east by the Alleghanies, is, in itself, to proclaim the writer a provincial. What is the West? What has it been in American life? To have the answers to these questions, is to understand the most significant features of the United States of to-day.

The West, at bottom, is a form of society, rather than an area. It is the term applied to the region whose social conditions result from the application of older institutions and ideas to the transforming influences of free land. By this application, a new environment is suddenly entered, freedom of opportunity is opened, the cake of custom is broken, and new activities, new lines of growth, new institutions and new ideals, are brought into existence. The wilderness disappears, the 'West' proper passes on to a new frontier, and in the former area, a new society has emerged from its contact with the backwoods. Gradually this society loses its primitive conditions, and assimilates itself to the type of the older social conditions of the East; but it bears within it enduring and distinguishing survivals of its frontier experience.

Decade after decade, West after West, this rebirth of American society has gone on, has left its traces behind it, and has reacted on the East. The history of our political institutions, our democracy, is not a history of imitation, of simple borrowing; it is a history of the evolution and adaptation of organs in response to changed environment, a history of the origin of new political species. In this sense, therefore, the West has been a constructive force of the highest significance in our life. To use the words of that acute and widely informed observer, Mr Bryce, 'The West is the most American part of America . . . What Europe is to Asia, what America is to England, that the Western States and Territories are to the Atlantic States.'

The West, as a phase of social organization, began with the Atlantic coast, and passed across the continent. But the colonial tide-water area was in close touch with the Old World, and soon lost its Western aspects. In the middle of the eighteenth century, the newer social conditions appeared along the upper waters of the tributaries of the Atlantic. Here it was that the West took on its distinguishing features, and transmitted frontier traits and ideals to this area in later days. On the coast, were the fishermen and skippers, the merchants and planters, with eyes turned toward Europe. Beyond the falls of the rivers were the pioneer farmers, largely of non-English stock, Scotch-Irish and German. They constituted a distinct people, and may be regarded as an expansion of the social and economic life of the middle region into the back country of the South. These frontiersmen were the ancestors of Boone, Andrew Jackson, Calhoun, Clay, and Lincoln. Washington and Jefferson were profoundly affected by these frontier conditions. The forest clearings have been the seed plots of American character.

In the Revolutionary days, the settlers crossed the Alleghanies and put a barrier between them and the coast. They became, to use their phrases, 'the men of the Western waters,' the heirs of the 'Western world.' In this era, the backwoodsmen, all along the western slopes of the mountains, with a keen sense of the difference between them and the dwellers on the coast, demanded organization into independent States of the Union. Self-government was their ideal. Said one of their rude, but energetic petitions for statehood: 'Some of our fellow-citizens may think we are not able to conduct our affairs and consult our interests; but if our society is rude, much wisdom is not necessary to supply our wants, and a fool can sometimes put on his clothes better than a wise man can do it for him.' This forest philosophy is the philosophy of American democracy. But the men of the coast were not ready to admit its implications. They apportioned the State legislatures so that the property-holding minority of the tidewater lands were able to out vote the more populous back countries. A similar system was proposed by Federalists in the constitutional convention of 1787. Gouverneur Morris, arguing in favor of basing representation on property as well as numbers, declared that 'he looked forward, also, to that range of new States which would soon be formed in the West. He thought the rule of representation ought to be so fixed, as to secure to the Atlantic States a prevalence in the national councils.' 'The new States,' said he, 'will know less of the public interest than these; will have an interest in many respects different; in particular will be little scrupulous of involving the community in wars, the burdens and operations of which would fall chiefly on the maritime States. Provision ought, therefore, to be made to prevent the maritime States from being hereafter outvoted by them.' He added that the Western country 'would not be able to furnish men equally enlightened to share in the administration of our common interests. The busy haunts of men, not the remote wilderness, was the proper school of political talents. If the Western people get power into their hands, they will ruin the Atlantic interest. The back members are always most averse to the best measures.' Add to these utterances of Gouverneur Morris the impassioned protest of Josiah Quincy, of Massachusetts, in the debates in the House of Representatives, on the admission of Louisiana. Referring to the discussion over the slave votes and the West in the constitutional convention, he declared, 'Suppose, then, that it had been distinctly foreseen that, in addition to the effect of this weight, the whole population of a world beyond the Mississippi was to be brought into this and the other branch of the legislature, to form our laws, control our rights, and decide our destiny. Sir, can it be pretended that the patriots of that day would for one moment have listened to it? . . . They had not taken degrees at the hospital of idiocy . . . Why, sir, I have already heard of six States, and some say there will be, at no great distant time, more. I have also heard that the mouth of the Ohio will be far to the east of the center of the contemplated empire . . . You have no authority to throw the rights and property of this people into "hotch-pot" with the wild men on the Missouri, nor with the mixed, though more respectable, race of Anglo-Hispano-Gallo-Americans who bask on the sands in the mouth of the Mississippi . . . Do you suppose the people of the Northern and Atlantic States will, or ought to, look on with patience and see Representatives and Senators from the Red River and Missouri, pouring themselves upon this and the other floor, managing the concerns of a seaboard fifteen hundred miles, at least, from their residence; and having a preponderancy in councils into which, constitutionally, they could never have been admitted?'

Like an echo from the fears expressed by the East at the close of the eighteenth century come the words of an eminent Eastern man of letters at the end of the nineteenth century, in warning against the West: 'Materialized in their temper; with few ideals of an ennobling sort; little instructed in the lessons of history; safe from exposure to the direct calamities and physical horrors of war; with undeveloped imaginations and sympathies – they form a community unfortunate and dangerous from the possession of power without a due sense of its corresponding responsibilities; a community in which the passion for war may easily be excited as the fancied means by which its greatness may be convincingly exhibited, and its ambitions gratified . . . Some chance spark may fire the prairie.'

Here, then, is the problem of the West, as it looked to New England leaders of thought in the beginning and at the end of this century. From the first, it was recognized that a new type was growing up beyond the seaboard, and that the time would come when the destiny of the nation would be in Western hands. The divergence of these societies became clear in the struggle over the ratification of the federal constitution. The up-country agricultural regions, the communities that were in debt and desired paper money, with some Western exceptions, opposed the instrument; but the areas of intercourse and property carried the day.

It is important to understand, therefore, what were some of the ideals of this early Western democracy. How did the frontiersman differ from the man of the coast?

The most obvious fact regarding the man of the Western Waters is that he had placed himself under influences destructive to many of the gains of civilization. Remote from the opportunity for systematic education, substituting a log hut in the forest-clearing for the social comforts of the town, he suffered hardships and privations, and reverted in many ways to primitive conditions of life. Engaged in a struggle to subdue the forest, working as an individual, and with little specie or capital, his interests were with the debtor class. At each stage of its advance, the West has favored an expansion of the currency. The pioneer had boundless confidence in the future of his own community, and when seasons of financial contraction and depression occurred, he, who had staked his all on confidence in Western development, and had fought the savage for his home, was inclined to reproach the conservative sections and classes. To explain this antagonism requires more than denunciation of dishonesty, ignorance, and boorishness as fundamental Western traits. Legislation in the United States has had to deal with two distinct social conditions. In some portions of the country there was, and is, an aggregation of property, and vested rights are in the foreground: in others, capital is lacking, more primitive conditions prevail, with different economic and social ideals, and the contentment of the average individual is placed in the foreground. That in the conflict between these two ideals an even hand has always been held by the government would be difficult to show.

The separation of the Western man from the seaboard, and his environment, made him in a large degree free from European precedents and forces. He looked at things independently and with small regard or appreciation for the best Old World experience. He had no ideal of a philosophical, eclectic nation, that should advance civilization by 'intercourse with foreigners and familiarity with their point of view, and readiness to adopt whatever is best and most suitable in their ideas, manners, and customs.' His was rather the ideal of conserving and developing what was original and valuable in this new country. The entrance of old society upon free lands meant to him opportunity for a new type of democracy and new popular ideals. The West was not conservative: buoyant self-confidence and self-assertion were distinguishing traits in its composition. It saw in its growth nothing less than a new order of society and state. In this conception were elements of evil and elements of good.

But the fundamental fact in regard to this new society was its relation to land. Professor Boutmy has said of the United States, 'Their one primary and predominant object is to cultivate and settle these prairies, forests, and vast waste lands. The striking and peculiar characteristic of American society is that it is not so much a democracy as a huge commercial company for the discovery, cultivation, and capitalization of its enormous territory. The United States are primarily a commercial society, and only secondarily a nation.' Of course, this involves a serious misapprehension. By the very fact of the task here set forth, far-reaching ideals of the state and of society have been evolved in the West, accompanied by loyalty to the nation representative of these ideals. But M. Boutmy's description hits the substantial fact, that the fundamental traits of the man of the interior were due to the free lands of the West. These turned his attention to the great task of subduing them to the purposes of civilization, and to the task of advancing his economic and social status in the new democracy which he was helping to create. Art, literature, refinement, scientific administration, all had to give way to this Titanic labor. Energy, incessant activity, became the lot of this new American. Says a traveler of the time of Andrew Jackson, 'America is like a vast workshop, over the door of which is printed in blazing characters, "No admittance here, except on business."' The West of our own day reminds Mr Bryce 'of the crowd which Vathek found in the hall of Eblis, each darting hither and thither with swift steps and unquiet mien, driven to and fro by a fire in the heart.

Time seems too short for what they have to do, and the result always to come short of their desire.'

But free lands and the consciousness of working out their social destiny did more than turn the Westerner to material interests and devote him to a restless existence. They promoted equality among the Western settlers, and reacted as a check on the aristocratic influences of the East. Where everybody could have a farm, almost for taking it, economic equality easily resulted, and this involved political equality. Not without a struggle would the Western man abandon this ideal, and it goes far to explain the unrest in the remote West to-day.

Western democracy included individual liberty, as well as equality. The frontiersman was impatient of restraints. He knew how to preserve order, even in the absence of legal authority. If there were cattle thieves, lynch law was sudden and effective: the regulators of the Carolinas were the predecessors of the claims associations of Iowa and the vigilance committees of California. But the individual was not ready to submit to complex regulations. Population was sparse, there was no multitude of jostling interests, as in older settlements, demanding an elaborate system of personal restraints. Society became atomic. There was a reproduction of the primitive idea of the personality of the law, a crime was more an offense against the victim than a violation of the law of the land. Substantial justice, secured in the most direct way, was the ideal of the backwoodsman. He had little patience with finely drawn distinctions or scruples of method. If the thing was one proper to

47

be done, then the most immediate, rough and ready, effective way was the best way.

It followed from the lack of organized political life, from the atomic conditions of the backwoods society, that the individual was exalted and given free play. The West was another name for opportunity. Here were mines to be seized, fertile valleys to be pre-empted, all the natural resources open to the shrewdest and the boldest. The United States is unique in the extent to which the individual has been given an open field, unchecked by restraints of an old social order, or of scientific administration of government. The self-made man was the Western man's ideal, was the kind of man that all men might become. Out of his wilderness experience, out of the freedom of his opportunities, he fashioned a formula for social regeneration – the freedom of the individual to seek his own. He did not consider that his conditions were exceptional and temporary.

Under such conditions, leadership easily develops – a leadership based on the possession of the qualities most serviceable to the young society. In the history of Western settlement, we see each forted village following its local hero. Clay, Jackson, Harrison, Lincoln, were illustrations of this tendency in periods when the Western hero rose to the dignity of national hero.

The Western man believed in the manifest destiny of his country. On his border, and checking his advance, were the Indian, the Spaniard, and the Englishman. He was indignant at Eastern indifference and lack of sympathy with his view of his relations to these peoples; at the short-sightedness of Eastern policy. The closure of the Mississippi by Spain, and the proposal to exchange our claim of freedom of navigating the river, in return for commercial advantages to New England, nearly led to the withdrawal of the West from the Union. It was the Western demands that brought about the purchase of Louisiana, and turned the scale in favor of declaring the War of 1812. Militant qualities were favored by the annual expansion of the settled area in the face of hostile Indians and the stubborn wilderness. The West caught the vision of the nation's continental destiny. Henry Adams, in his History of the United States, makes the American of 1800 exclaim to the foreign visitor, 'Look at my wealth! See these solid mountains of salt and iron, of lead, copper, silver, and gold. See these magnificent cities scattered broadcast to the Pacific! See my cornfields rustling and waving in the summer breeze from ocean to ocean, so far that the sun itself is not high enough to mark where the distant mountains bound my golden seas. Look at this continent of mine, fairest of created worlds, as she lies turning up to the sun's never failing caress her broad and exuberant breasts, overflowing with milk for her hundred million children.' And the foreigner saw only dreary deserts, tenanted by sparse, ague-stricken pioneers and savages. The cities were log huts and gambling dens. But the frontiersman's dream was prophetic. In spite of his rude, gross nature, this early Western man was an idealist withal. He dreamed dreams and beheld visions. He had faith in man, hope for democracy, belief in America's destiny, unbounded confidence in his ability to make his dreams come true. Said Harriet Martineau in 1834, 'I regard the American people as a great embryo poet, now moody, now wild, but bringing out results of absolute good sense: restless and wayward in action, but with deep peace at his heart; exulting that he has caught the true aspect of things past, and the depth of futurity which lies before him, wherein to create something so magnificent as the world has scarcely begun to dream of. There is the strongest hope of a nation that is capable of being possessed with an idea.'

It is important to bear this idealism of the West in mind. The very materialism that has been urged against the West was accompanied by ideals of equality, of the exaltation of the common man, of national expansion, that makes it a profound mistake to write of the West as though it were engrossed in mere material ends. It has been, and is, pre-eminently a region of ideals, mistaken or not.

It is obvious that these economic and social conditions were so fundamental in Western life that they might well dominate whatever accessions came to the West by immigration from the coast sections or from Europe. Nevertheless, the West cannot be understood without bearing in mind the fact that it has received the great streams from the North and from the South, and that the Mississippi compelled these currents to intermingle. Here it was that sectionalism first gave way under the pressure of unification. Ultimately the conflicting ideas and institutions of the old sections struggled for dominance in this area under the influence of the forces that made for uniformity, but this is merely another phase of the truth that the West must become unified, that it could not rest in sectional groupings. For precisely this reason the struggle occurred. In the period from the Revolution to the close of the War of 1812, the democracy of the Southern and Middle States contributed the main streams of settlement and social influence to the West. Even in Ohio political power was soon lost by the New England leaders. The democratic spirit of the Middle region left an indelible impress on the West in this its formative period. After the War of 1812, New England, its supremacy in the carrying trade of the world having vanished, became a hive from which swarms of settlers went out to western New York and the remoter regions.

These settlers spread New England ideals of education and character and political institutions, and acted as a leaven of great significance in the Northwest. But it would be a mistake to believe that an unmixed New England influence took possession of the Northwest. These pioneers did not come from the class that conserved the type of New England civilization pure and undefiled. They represented a less contented, less conservative influence. Moreover, by their sojourn in the Middle Region, on their westward march, they underwent modification, and when the farther West received them, they suffered a forest-change, indeed. The Westernized New England man was no longer the representative of the section that he left. He was less conservative, less provincial, more adaptable and approachable, less rigorous in his Puritan ideals, less a man of culture, more a man of action.

As might have been expected, therefore, the Western men, in the 'era of good feeling,' had much homogeneity throughout the Mississippi Valley, and began to stand as a new national type. Under the lead of Henry Clay they invoked the national government to break down the mountain barrier by internal improvements, and thus to give their crops an outlet to the coast. Under him they appealed to the national government for a protective tariff to create a home market. A group of frontier States entered the Union with democratic provisions respecting the suffrage, and with devotion to the nation that had given them their lands, built their roads and canals, regulated their territorial life, and made them equals in the sisterhood of States. At last these Western forces of aggressive nationalism and democracy took possession of the government in the person of the man who best embodied them, Andrew Jackson. This new democracy that captured the country and destroyed the ideals of statesmanship came from no theorist's dreams of the German forest. It came, stark and strong and full of life, from the American forest. But the triumph of this Western democracy revealed also the fact that it could rally to its aid the laboring classes of the coast, then just beginning to acquire self-consciousness and organization.

The next phase of Western development revealed forces of division between the northern and southern portions of the West. With the spread of the cotton culture went the slave system and the great plantation. The small farmer in his log cabin, raising varied crops, was displaced by the planter raising cotton. In all except the mountainous areas the industrial organization of the tidewater took possession of the Southwest, the unity of the back country was broken, and the solid South was formed. In the Northwest this was the era of railroads and canals, opening the region to the increasing stream of Middle State and New England settlement, and strengthening the opposition to slavery. A map showing the location of the men of New England ancestry in the Northwest would represent also the counties in which the Free Soil party cast its heaviest votes. The commercial connections of the Northwest likewise were reversed by the railroad. The result is stated by a writer in *De Bow's Review* in 1852 in these words: –

'What is New Orleans now? Where are her dreams of greatness and glory? . . . Whilst she slept, an enemy has sowed tares in her most prolific fields. Armed with energy, enterprise, and an indomitable spirit, that enemy, by a system of bold, vigorous, and sustained efforts, has succeeded in reversing the very laws of nature and of nature's God, – rolled back the mighty tide of the Mississippi and its thousand tributary streams, until their mouth, practically and commercially, is more at New York or Boston than at New Orleans.'

The West broke asunder, and the great struggle over the social system to be given to the lands beyond the Mississippi followed. In the Civil War the Northwest furnished the national hero – Lincoln was the very flower of frontier training and ideals – and it also took into its hands the whole power of the government. Before the war closed, the West could claim the President, Vice-President, Chief Justice, Speaker of the House, Secretary of the Treasury, Postmaster-General, Attorney-General, General of the army, and Admiral of the navy. The leading generals of the war had been furnished by the

West. It was the region of action, and in the crisis it took the reins.

The triumph of the nation was followed by a new era of Western development. The national forces projected themselves across the prairies and plains. Railroads, fostered by government loans and land grants, opened the way for settlement and poured a flood of European immigrants and restless pioneers from all sections of the Union into the government lands. The army of the United States pushed back the Indian, rectangular Territories were carved into checkerboard States, creations of the federal government, without a history, without physiographical unity, without particularistic ideas. The later frontiersman leaned on the strong arm of national power.

At the same time the South underwent a revolution. The plantation, based on slavery, gave place to the farm, the gentry to the democratic elements. As in the West, new industries, of mining and of manufacture, sprang up as by magic. The New South, like the New West, was an area of construction, a debtor area, an area of unrest; and it, too, had learned the uses to which federal legislation might be put.

In the meantime the Old Northwest[2] passed through an economic and social transformation. The whole West furnished an area over which successive waves of economic development have passed. The State of Wisconsin, now much like parts of the State of New York, was at

[2] The present States of Ohio, Indiana, Illinois, Michigan, and Wisconsin.

an earlier period like the State of Nebraska of to-day; the Granger movement and Greenback party had for a time the ascendancy; and in the northern counties of the State, where there is a sparser population, and the country is being settled, its sympathies are still with the debtor class. Thus the Old Northwest is a region where the older frontier conditions survive in parts, and where the inherited ways of looking at things are largely to be traced to its frontier days. At the same time it is a region in many ways assimilated to the East. It understands both sections. It is not entirely content with the existing structure of economic society in the sections where wealth has accumulated and corporate organizations are powerful; but neither has it seemed to feel that its interests lie in supporting the program of the prairies and the South. In the Fifty-third Congress it voted for the income tax, but it rejected free coinage. It is still affected by the ideal of the self-made man, rather than by the ideal of industrial nationalism. It is more American, but less cosmopolitan than the seaboard.

We are now in a position to see clearly some of the factors involved in the Western problem. For nearly three centuries the dominant fact in American life has been expansion. With the settlement of the Pacific coast and the occupation of the free lands, this movement has come to a check. That these energies of expansion will no longer operate would be a rash prediction; and the demands for a vigorous foreign policy, for an interoceanic canal, for a revival of our power upon the seas, and for the extension of American influence to outlying islands and adjoining countries, are indications that the movement will continue. The stronghold of these demands lies west of the Alleghanies.

In the remoter West, the restless, rushing wave of settlement has broken with a shock against the arid plains. The free lands are gone, the continent is crossed, and all this push and energy is turning into channels of agitation. Failures in one area can no longer be made good by taking up land on a new frontier; the conditions of a settled society are being reached with suddenness and with confusion. The West has been built up with borrowed capital, and the question of the stability of gold, as a standard of deferred payments, is eagerly agitated by the debtor West, profoundly dissatisfied with the industrial conditions that confront it, and actuated by frontier directness and rigor in its remedies. For the most part, the men who built up the West beyond the Mississippi, and who are now leading the agitation, came as pioneers from the old Northwest, in the days when it was just passing from the stage of a frontier section. For example, Senator Allen of Nebraska, president of the recent national Populist Convention, and a type of the political leaders of his section, was born in Ohio in the middle of the century, went in his youth to Iowa, and not long after the Civil War made his home in Nebraska. As a boy, he saw the buffalo driven out by the settlers; he saw the Indian retreat as the pioneer advanced. His training is that of the old West, in its frontier days. And now the frontier opportunities are gone. Discontent is demanding an extension of governmental activity in its behalf. In these demands, it finds itself in touch with the depressed agricultural classes and the working men of the South and East. The Western problem is no longer a sectional problem: it is a social problem on a national scale. The greater West, extending from the Alleghanies to the Pacific, cannot be regarded as a unit; it requires analysis into regions and classes. But its area, its population, and its material resources would give force to its assertion that if there is a sectionalism in the country, the sectionalism is Eastern. The old West, united to the new South, would produce, not a new sectionalism, but a new Americanism. It would not mean sectional disunion, as some have speculated, but it might mean a drastic assertion of national government and imperial expansion under a popular hero.

This, then, is the real situation: a people composed of heterogeneous materials, with diverse and conflicting ideals and social interests, having passed from the task of filling up the vacant spaces of the continent, is now thrown back upon itself, and is seeking an equilibrium. The diverse elements are being fused into national unity. The forces of reorganization are turbulent and the nation seems like a witches' kettle.

But the West has its own centers of industrial life and culture not unlike those of the East. It has State universities, rivaling in conservative and scientific economic instruction those of any other part of the Union, and its citizens more often visit the East, than do Eastern men the West. As time goes on, its industrial development will bring it more into harmony with the East.

Moreover, the Old Northwest holds the balance of power, and is the battlefield on which these issues of American development are to be settled. It has more in common with all parts of the nation than has any other region. It understands the East, as the East does not understand the West. The White City which recently rose on the shores of Lake Michigan fitly typified its growing culture as well as its capacity for great achievement. Its complex and representative industrial organization and business ties, its determination to hold fast to what is original and good in its Western experience, and its readiness to learn and receive the results of the experience of other sections and nations, make it an open-minded and safe arbiter of the American destiny.

In the long run the 'Center of the Republic' may be trusted to strike a wise balance between the contending ideals. But she does not deceive herself; she knows that the problem of the West means nothing less than the problem of working out original social ideals and social adjustments for the American nation.

III

The Significance of the Mississippi Valley in American History (1909–10)

The rise of a company of sympathetic and critical students of history in the South and in the West is bound to revolutionize the perspective of American history. Already our Eastern colleagues are aware in general, if not in detail, of the importance of the work of this nation in dealing with the vast interior, and with the influence of the West upon the nation. Indeed, I might take as the text for this address the words of one of our Eastern historians, Professor Albert Bushnell Hart, who, a decade ago, wrote:

The Mississippi Valley yields to no region in the world in interest, in romance, and in promise for the future. Here, if anywhere, is the real America – the field, the theater, and the basis of the civilization of the Western World. The history of the Mississippi Valley is the history of the United States; its future is the future of one of the most powerful of modern nations.

If those of us who have been insisting on the importance of our own region are led at times by the enthusiasm of the pioneer for the inviting historical domain that opens before us to overstate the importance of our subject, we may at least plead that we have gone no farther than some of our brethren of the East; and we may take comfort in this declaration of Theodore Roosevelt:

The states that have grown up around the Great Lakes and in the Valley of the Upper Mississippi, [are] the states which are destined to be the greatest, the richest, the most prosperous of all the great, rich, and prosperous commonwealths which go to make up the mightiest republic the world has ever seen. These states . . . form the heart of the country geographically, and they will soon become the heart in population and in political and social importance . . . I should be sorry to think that before these states there loomed a future of material prosperity merely. I regard this section of the country as the heart of true American sentiment.

In studying the history of the whole Mississippi Valley, therefore, the members of this Association are study-ing the origins of that portion of the nation which is admitted by competent Eastern authorities to be the section potentially most influential in the future of America. They are also studying the region which has engaged the most vital activities of the whole nation; for the problems arising from the existence of the Mississippi Valley, whether of movement of population, diplomacy, politics, economic development, or social structure, have been fundamental problems in shaping the nation. It is not a narrow, not even a local, interest which determines the mission of this Association. It is nothing less than the study of the American people in the presence and under the influence of the vast spaces, the imperial resources of the great interior. The social destiny of this Valley will be the social destiny, and will mark the place in history, of the United States.

In a large sense, and in the one usually given to it by geographers and historians, the Mississippi Valley includes the whole interior basin, a province which drains into nearly two thousand miles of navigable waters of the Mississippi itself, two thousand miles of the tawny flood of the Missouri, and a thousand miles of the Ohio – five thousand miles of main water highways open to the steamboat, nearly two and a half million square miles of drainage basin, a land greater than all Europe except Russia, Norway, and Sweden, a land of levels, marked by essential geographic unity, a land estimated to be able to support a population of two or three hundred millions, three times the present population of the whole nation, an empire of natural resources in which to build a noble social structure worthy to hold its place as the heart of American industrial, political and spiritual life.

The significance of the Mississippi Valley in American history was first shown in the fact that it opened to various nations visions of power in the New World – visions that sweep across the horizon of historical possibility like the luminous but unsubstantial aurora of a comet's train, portentous and fleeting.

Out of the darkness of the primitive history of the continent are being drawn the evidences of the rise and fall of Indian cultures, the migrations through and into the great Valley by men of the Stone Age, hinted at in legends and languages, dimly told in the records of mounds and artifacts, but waiting still for complete interpretation.

Into these spaces and among the savage peoples, came France and wrote a romantic page in our early history, a page that tells of unfulfilled empire. What is striking in the effect of the Mississippi Valley upon France is the pronounced influence of the unity of its great spaces. It is not without meaning that Radisson and Groseilliers not only reached the extreme of Lake Superior but also, in all probability, entered upon the waters of the Mississippi and learned of its western affluent; that Marquette not only received the Indians of the Illinois region in his post on the shores of Lake Superior, but traversed the length of the Mississippi almost to its mouth, and returning revealed the site of Chicago; that La Salle was inspired with the vision of a huge interior empire reaching from the Gulf to the Great Lakes. Before the close of the seventeenth century, Perrot's influence was supreme in the Upper Mississippi, while D'Iberville was laying the foundations of Louisiana toward the mouth of the river. Nor is it without significance that while the Verendryes were advancing toward the northwest (where they discovered the Big Horn Mountains and revealed the natural boundaries of the Valley) the Mallet brothers were ascending the Platte, crossing the Colorado plains to Santa Fé and so revealing the natural boundaries toward the southwest.

To the English the great Valley was a land beyond the Alleghanies. Spotswood, the far-sighted Governor of Virginia, predecessor of frontier builders, grasped the situation when he proposed western settlements to prevent the French from becoming a great people at the back of the colonies. He realized the importance of the Mississippi Valley as the field for expansion, and the necessity to the English empire of dominating it, if England would remain the great power of the New World.

In the war that followed between France and England, we now see what the men of the time could not have realized: that the main issue was neither the possession of the fisheries nor the approaches to the St Lawrence on the one hemisphere, nor the possession of India on the other, but the mastery of the interior basin of North America.

How little the nations realized the true meaning of the final victory of England is shown in the fact that Spain reluctantly received from France the cession of the lands beyond the Mississippi, accepting it as a means of preventing the infringement of her colonial monopoly in Spanish America rather than as a field for imperial expansion.

But we know now that when George Washington came as a stripling to the camp of the French at the edge of the great Valley and demanded the relinquishment of the French posts in the name of Virginia, he was demanding in the name of the English-speaking people the right to occupy and rule the real center of American resources and power. When Braddock's axmen cut their road from the Potomac toward the forks of the Ohio they were opening a channel through which the forces of civilization should flow with ever increasing momentum and 'carving a cross on the wilderness rim' at the spot which is now the center of industrial power of the American nation.

England trembled on the brink of her great conquest, fearful of the effect of these far-stretching rivers upon her colonial system, timorous in the presence of the fierce peoples who held the vast domain beyond the Alleghanies. It seems clear, however, that the Proclamation of 1763, forbidding settlement and the patenting of lands beyond the Alleghanies, was not intended as a permanent creation of an Indian reservation out of this Valley, but was rather a temporary arrangement in order that British plans might mature and a system of gradual colonization be devised. Already our greatest leaders, men like Washington and Franklin, had been quick to see the importance of this new area for enlarged activities of the American people. A sudden revelation that it was the West, rather than the ocean, which was the real theater for the creative energy of America came with the triumph over France. The Ohio Company and the Loyal Land Company indicate the interest at the outbreak of the war, while the Mississippi Company, headed by the Washingtons and Lees, organized to occupy southern Illinois, Indiana, and western Kentucky, mark the Virginia interest in the Mississippi Valley, and Franklin's activity in promoting a colony in the Illinois country illustrates the interest of the Philadelphians. Indeed, Franklin saw clearly the possibilities of a settlement there as a means of breaking up Spanish America. Writing to his son in 1767 he declared that a 'settlement should be made in the Illinois country . . . raising a strength there which on occasions of a future war might easily be poured down the Mississippi upon the lower country and into the Bay of Mexico to be used against Cuba, the French Islands, or Mexico itself.'

The Mississippi Valley had been the despair of France in the matter of governmental control. The coureurs de bois escaping from restraints of law and order took their way through its extensive wilderness, exploring and trading as they listed. Similarly, when the English colonists crossed the Alleghanies they escaped from the control of mother colonies as well as of the mother country. If the Mississippi Valley revealed to the statesmen of the East, in the exultation of the war with France, an opportunity for new empire building, it revealed to the frontiersmen, who penetrated the passes of the Alleghanies, and entered into their new inheritance, the sharp distinctions between them and the Eastern lands which they left behind. From the beginning it was clear that the lands beyond the Alleghanies furnished an opportunity and an incentive to develop American society on independent and unconventional lines. The 'men of the Western Waters' broke with the old order of things, subordinated social restraint to the freedom of the individual, won their title to the rich lands which they entered by hard fighting against the Indians, hotly challenged the right of the East to rule them, demanded their own States, and would not be refused, spoke with contempt of the old social order of ranks and classes in the lands between the Alleghanies and the Atlantic, and proclaimed the ideal of democracy for the vast country which they had entered. Not with the mercurial facility of the French did they follow the river systems of the Great Valley. Like the advance of the glacier they changed the face of the country in their steady and inevitable progress, and they sought the sea. It was not long before the Spaniards at the mouth of the river realized the meaning of the new forces that had entered the Valley.

In 1794 the Governor of Louisiana wrote:

This vast and restless population progressively driving the Indian tribes before them and upon us, seek to possess themselves of all the extensive regions which the Indians occupy between the Ohio and Mississippi rivers, the Gulf of Mexico, and the Appalachian Mountains, thus becoming our neighbors, at the same time that they menacingly ask for the free navigation of the Mississippi. If they achieve their object, their ambitions would not be confined to this side of the Mississippi. Their writings, public papers, and speeches, all turn on this point, the free navigation of the Gulf by the rivers . . . which empty into it, the rich fur trade of the Missouri, and in time the possession of the rich mines of the interior provinces of the very Kingdom of Mexico. Their mode of growth and their policy are as formidable for Spain as their armies . . . Their roving spirit and the readiness with which they procure sustenance and shelter facilitate rapid settlement. A rifle and a little corn meal in a bag are enough for an American wandering alone in the woods for a month . . . With logs crossed upon one another he makes a house, and even an impregnable fort against the Indians . . . Cold does not terrify him, and when a family wearies of one place, it moves to another and settles there with the same ease.

If such men come to occupy the banks of the Mississippi and Missouri, or secure their navigation, doubtless nothing will prevent them from crossing and penetrating into our provinces on the other side, which, being to a great extent unoccupied, can oppose no resistance . . . In my opinion, a general revolution in America threatens Spain unless the remedy be applied promptly.

In fact, the pioneers who had occupied the uplands of the South, the backwoods stock with its Scotch-Irish leaders which had formed on the eastern edge of the Alleghanies, separate and distinct from the type of tide-water and New England, had found in the Mississippi Valley a new field for expansion under conditions of free land and unrestraint. These conditions gave it promise of ample time to work out its own social type. But, first of all, these men who were occupying the Western Waters must find an outlet for their surplus products, if they were to become a powerful people. While the Alleghanies placed a veto toward the east, the Mississippi opened a broad highway to the south. Its swift current took their flat boats in its strong arms to bear them to the sea, but across the outlet of the great river Spain drew the barrier of her colonial monopoly and denied them exit.

The significance of the Mississippi Valley in American history at the opening of the new republic, therefore, lay in the fact that, beyond the area of the social and political control of the thirteen colonies, there had arisen a new and aggressive society which imperiously put the questions of the public lands, internal communication, local self-government, defense, and aggressive expansion, before the legislators of the old colonial régime. The men of the Mississippi Valley compelled the men of the East to think in American terms instead of European. They dragged a reluctant nation on in a new course.

From the Revolution to the end of the War of 1812 Europe regarded the destiny of the Mississippi Valley as undetermined. Spain desired to maintain her hold by means of the control given through the possession of the mouth of the river and the Gulf, by her influence upon the Indian tribes, and by intrigues with the settlers. Her object was primarily to safeguard the Spanish American monopoly which had made her a great nation in the world. Instinctively she seemed to surmise that out of this Valley were the issues of her future; here was the lever which might break successively, from her empire fragments about the Gulf – Louisiana, Florida and Texas, Cuba and Porto Rico – the Southwest and Pacific coast, and even the Philippines and the Isthmian Canal, while the American republic, building itself on the resources of the Valley, should become paramount over the independent republics into which her empire was to disintegrate.

France, seeking to regain her former colonial power, would use the Mississippi Valley as a means of provisioning her West Indian islands; of dominating Spanish America, and of subordinating to her purposes the feeble United States, which her policy assigned to the lands between the Atlantic and the Alleghanies. The ancient

Bourbon monarchy, the revolutionary republic, and the Napoleonic empire – all contemplated the acquisition of the whole Valley of the Mississippi from the Alleghanies to the Rocky Mountains.

England holding the Great Lakes, dominating the northern Indian populations and threatening the Gulf and the mouth of the Mississippi by her fleet, watched during the Revolution, the Confederation, and the early republic for the breaking of the fragile bonds of the thirteen States, ready to extend her protection over the settlers in the Mississippi Valley.

Alarmed by the prospect of England's taking Louisiana and Florida from Spain, Jefferson wrote in 1790: 'Embraced from St Croix to St Mary's on one side by their possessions, on the other by their fleet, we need not hesitate to say that they would soon find means to unite to them all the territory covered by the ramifications of the Mississippi.' And that, he thought, must result in 'bloody and eternal war or indissoluble confederacy' with England.

None of these nations deemed it impossible that American settlers in the Mississippi Valley might be won to accept another flag than that of the United States. Gardoqui had the effrontery in 1787 to suggest to Madison that the Kentuckians would make good Spanish subjects. France enlisted the support of frontiersmen led by George Rogers Clark for her attempted conquest of Louisiana in 1793. England tried to win support among the western settlers. Indeed, when we recall that George Rogers Clark accepted a commission as Major General from France in 1793 and again in 1798; that Wilkinson, afterwards commander-in-chief of the American army, secretly asked Spanish citizenship and promised renunciation of his American allegiance; that Governor Sevier of Franklin, afterwards Senator from Tennessee and its first Governor as a State, Robertson the founder of Cumberland, and Blount, Governor of the Southwest Territory and afterwards Senator from Tennessee, were all willing to accept the rule of another nation sooner than see the navigation of the Mississippi yielded by the American government we can easily believe that it lay within the realm of possibility that another allegiance might have been accepted by the frontiersmen themselves. We may well trust Rufus Putnam, whose federalism and devotion to his country had been proved and whose work in founding New England's settlement at Marietta is well known, when he wrote in 1790 in answer to Fisher Ames's question whether the Mississippi Valley could be retained in the Union: 'Should Congress give up her claim to the navigation of the Mississippi or cede it to the Spaniards, I believe the people in the Western quarter would separate themselves from the United States very soon. Such a measure, I have no doubt, would excite so much rage and dissatisfaction that the people would sooner put themselves under the despotic government of Spain than remain the indented servants of Congress.' He added that if Congress did not afford due protection also to these western settlers they might turn to England or Spain.

Prior to the railroad the Mississippi Valley was potentially the basis for an independent empire, in spite of the fact that its population would inevitably be drawn from the Eastern States. Its natural outlet was down the current to the Gulf. New Orleans controlled the Valley, in the words of Wilkinson, 'as the key the lock, or the citadel the outworks.' So long as the Mississippi Valley was menaced, or in part controlled, by rival European states, just so long must the United States be a part of the state system of Europe, involved in its fortunes. And particularly was this the case in view of the fact that until the Union made internal commerce, based upon the Mississippi Valley, its dominant economic interest, the merchants and sailors of the northeastern States and the staple producers of the southern sea-board were a commercial appanage of Europe. The significance of the Mississippi Valley was clearly seen by Jefferson. Writing to Livingston in 1802 he declared:

There is on the globe one single spot, the possessor of which is our natural and habitual enemy. It is New Orleans, through which the produce of three-eights of our territory must pass to market, and from its fertility it will ere long yield more than half of our whole produce and contain more than half of our inhabitants . . . The day that France takes possession of New Orleans fixes the sentence which is to restrain her within her low-water mark. It seals the union of two nations who in conjunction can maintain exclusive possession of the ocean. From that moment we must marry ourselves to the British fleet and nation . . . holding the two continents of America in sequestration for the common purposes of the united British and American nations.

The acquisition of Louisiana was a recognition of the essential unity of the Mississippi Valley. The French engineer Collot reported to his government after an investigation in 1796:

All the positions on the left [east] bank of the Mississippi . . . without the alliance of the Western states are far from covering Louisiana . . . When two nations possess, one the coasts and the other the plains, the former must inevitably embark or submit. From thence I conclude that the Western States of the North American republic must unite themselves with Louisiana and form in the future one single compact nation; or else that colony to whatever power it shall belong will be conquered or devoured.

The effect of bringing political unity to the Mississippi Valley by the Louisiana Purchase was profound. It was the decisive step of the United States on an independent career as a world power, free from entangling foreign alliances. The victories of Harrison in the Northwest, in the War of 1812 that followed, ensured our expansion in the northern half of the Valley. Jackson's triumphal march to the Gulf and his defense of New Orleans in the same war won the basis for that Cotton Kingdom, so important in the economic life of the nation and so pregnant with the issue of slavery. The acquisition of Florida, Texas, and the Far West followed naturally. Not only was the nation set on an independent path in foreign relations; its political system was revolutionized, for the Mississippi Valley now opened the way for adding State after State, swamping the New England section and its Federalism. The doctrine of strict construction had received a fatal blow at the hands of its own prophet. The old conception of historic sovereign States, makers of a federation, was shattered by this vast addition of raw material for an indefinite number of parallelograms called States, nursed through a Territorial period by the Federal government, admitted under conditions, and animated by national rather than by State patriotism.

The area of the nation had been so enlarged and the development of the internal resources so promoted, by the acquisition of the whole course of the mighty river, its tributaries and its outlet, that the Atlantic coast soon turned its economic energies from the sea to the interior. Cities and sections began to struggle for ascendancy over its industrial life. A real national activity, a genuine American culture began. The vast spaces, the huge natural resources, of the Valley demanded exploitation and population. Later there came the tide of foreign immigration which has risen so steadily that it has made a composite American people whose amalgamation is destined to produce a new national stock.

But without attempting to exhaust, or even to indicate, all the effects of the Louisiana Purchase, I wish next to ask your attention to the significance of the Mississippi Valley in the promotion of democracy and the transfer of the political center of gravity in the nation. The Mississippi Valley has been the especial home of democracy. Born of free land and the pioneer spirit, nurtured in the ideas of the Revolution and finding free play for these ideas in the freedom of the wilderness, democracy showed itself in the earliest utterances of the men of the Western Waters and it has persisted there. The demand for local self-government, which was insistent on the frontier, and the endorsement given by the Alleghanies to these demands led to the creation of a system of independent Western governments and to the Ordinance of 1787, an original contribution to colonial policy. This was framed in the period when any rigorous subjection of the West to Eastern rule would have endangered the ties that bound them to the Union itself. In the Constitutional Convention prominent Eastern statesmen expressed their fears of the Western democracy and would have checked its ability to out-vote the regions of property by limiting its political power, so that it should never equal that of the Atlantic coast. But more liberal counsels prevailed. In the first debates upon the public lands, also, it was clearly stated that the social system of the nation was involved quite as much as the question of revenue. Eastern fears that cheap lands in abundance would depopulate the Atlantic States and check their industrial growth by a scarcity of labor supply were met by the answer of one of the representatives in 1796:

I question if any man would be hardy enough to point out a class of citizens by name that ought to be the servants of the community; yet unless that is done to what class of the People could you direct such a law? But if you passed such an act [limiting the area offered for sale in the Mississippi Valley], it would be tantamount to saying that there is some class which must remain here, and by law be obliged to serve the others for such wages as they please to give.

Gallatin showed his comprehension of the basis of the prosperous American democracy in the same debate when he said:

If the cause of the happiness of this country was examined into, it would be found to arise as much from the great plenty of land in proportion to the inhabitants, which their citizens enjoyed as from the wisdom of their political institutions.

Out of this frontier democratic society where the freedom and abundance of land in the great Valley opened a refuge to the oppressed in all regions, came the Jacksonian democracy which governed the nation after the downfall of the party of John Quincy Adams. Its center rested in Tennessee, the region from which so large a portion of the Mississippi Valley was settled by descendants of the men of the Upland South. The rule of the Mississippi Valley is seen when we recall the place that Tennessee, Kentucky, and Missouri held in both parties. Besides Jackson, Clay, Harrison and Polk, we count such presidential candidates as Hugh White and John Bell, Vice President R. M. Johnson, Grundy, the chairman of the finance committee, and Benton, the champion of western radicalism.

It was in this same period, and largely by reason of the drainage of population to the West, and the stir in the air raised by the Western winds of Jacksonian democracy, that most of the older States reconstructed their constitutions on a more democratic basis. From the Mississippi Valley where there were liberal suffrage provisions (based on population alone instead of property and population), disregard of vested interests, and insistence on the rights of man, came the inspiration for this era of change in the franchise and apportionment, of reform of laws for imprisonment for debt, of general attacks upon monopoly and privilege. 'It is now plain,' wrote Jackson in 1837, 'that the war is to be carried on by the monied aristocracy of the few against the democracy of numbers; the [prosperous] to make the honest laborers hewers of wood and drawers of water . . . through the credit and paper system.'

By this time the Mississippi Valley had grown in population and political power so that it ranked with the older sections. The next indication of its significance in American history which I shall mention is its position in shaping the economic and political course of the nation between the close of the War of 1812 and the slavery struggle. In 1790 the Mississippi Valley had a population of about a hundred thousand, or one-fortieth of that of the United States as a whole; by 1810 it had over a million, or one-seventh; by 1830 it had three and two-thirds millions, or over one-fourth; by 1840 over six millions, more than one-third. While the Atlantic coast increased only a million and a half souls between 1830 and 1840, the Mississippi Valley gained nearly three millions. Ohio (virgin wilderness in 1790) was, half a century later, nearly as populous as Pennsylvania and twice as populous as Massachusetts. While Virginia, North Carolina, and South Carolina were gaining 60,000 souls between 1830 and 1840, Illinois gained 318,000. Indeed, the growth of this State alone excelled that of the entire South Atlantic States.

These figures show the significance of the Mississippi Valley in its pressure upon the older section by the competition of its cheap lands, its abundant harvests, and its drainage of the labor supply. All of these things meant an upward lift to the Eastern wage earner. But they meant also an increase of political power in the Valley. Before the War of 1812 the Mississippi Valley had six senators, New England ten, the Middle States ten, and the South eight. By 1840 the Mississippi Valley had twenty-two senators, double those of the Middle States and New England combined, and nearly three times as many as the Old South; while in the House of Representatives the Mississippi Valley outweighed any one of the old sections. In 1810 it had less than one-third the power of New England and the South together in the House. In 1840 it outweighed them both combined and because of its special circumstances it held the balance of power.

While the Mississippi Valley thus rose to superior political power as compared with any of the old sections, its economic development made it the inciting factor in the industrial life of the nation. After the War of 1812 the steamboat revolutionized the transportation facilities of the Mississippi Valley. In each economic area a surplus formed, demanding an outlet and demanding returns in manufactures. The spread of cotton into the lower Mississippi Valley and the Gulf Plains had a double significance. This transfer of the center of cotton production away from the Atlantic South not only brought increasing hardship and increasing unrest to the East as the competition of the virgin soils depressed Atlantic land values and made Eastern labor increasingly dear, but the price of cotton fell also in due proportion to the increase in production by the Mississippi Valley. While the transfer of economic power from the Seaboard South to the Cotton Kingdom of the lower Mississippi Valley was in progress, the upper Mississippi Valley was leaping forward, partly under the stimulus of a market for its surplus in the plantations of the South, where almost exclusive cultivation of the great staples resulted in a lack of foodstuffs and livestock.

At the same time the great river and its affluents became the highway of a commerce that reached to the West Indies, the Atlantic Coast, Europe, and South America. The Mississippi Valley was an industrial entity, from Pittsburgh and Santa Fé to New Orleans. It became the most important influence in American politics and industry. Washington had declared in 1784 that it was the part of wisdom for Virginia to bind the West to the East by ties of interest through internal improvement thereby taking advantage of the extensive and valuable trade of a rising empire.

This realization of the fact that an economic empire was growing up beyond the mountains stimulated rival cities, New York, Philadelphia, and Baltimore, to engage in a struggle to supply the West with goods and receive its products. This resulted in an attempt to break down the barrier of the Alleghanies by internal improvements. The movement became especially active after the War of 1812, when New York carried out De Witt Clinton's vast conception of making by the Erie Canal a greater Hudson which should drain to the port of New York all the basin of the Great Lakes, and by means of other canals even divert the traffic from the tributaries of the Mississippi. New York City's commercial ascendancy dates from this connection with interior New York and the Mississippi Valley. A writer in Hunt's *Merchants' Magazine* in 1869 makes the significance of this clearer by these words:

There was a period in the history of the seaboard cities when there was no West; and when the Alleghany Mountains formed the frontier of settlement and agricultural production. During that epoch the seaboard cities, North and South, grew in proportion to the extent and fertility of the country in their rear; and as Maryland, Virginia, the Carolinas and Georgia were more productive in staples valuable to commerce than the colonies north of them, the cities of Baltimore, Norfolk, Charleston, and Savannah enjoyed a greater trade and experienced a larger growth than those on the northern seaboard.

He, then, classifies the periods of city development into three: (1) the provincial, limited to the Atlantic seaboard; (2) that of canal and turnpike connected with the Mississippi Valley; and (3) that of railroad connection. Thus he was able to show how Norfolk, for example, was shut off from the enriching currents of interior trade and was outstripped by New York. The efforts of Philadelphia, Baltimore, Charleston, and Savannah to divert the trade of the Mississippi system to their own ports on the Atlantic, and the rise or fall of these cities in proportion as they succeeded are a sufficient indication of the meaning of the Mississippi Valley in American industrial life. What colonial empire has been for London that the Mississippi Valley is to the seaboard cities of the United States, awakening visions of industrial empire, systematic control of vast spaces, producing the American type of the captain of industry.

It was not alone city rivalry that converged upon the Mississippi Valley and sought its alliance. Sectional rivalry likewise saw that the balance of power possessed by the interior furnished an opportunity for combinations. This was a fundamental feature of Calhoun's policy when he urged the seaboard South to complete a railroad system to tap the Northwest. As Washington had hoped to make western trade seek its outlet in Virginia and build up the industrial power of the Old Dominion by enriching intercourse with the Mississippi Valley, as Monroe wished to bind the West to Virginia's political interests; and as De Witt Clinton wished to attach it to New York, so Calhoun and Hayne would make 'Georgia and Carolina the commercial center of the Union, and the two most powerful and influential members of the confederacy,' by draining the Mississippi Valley to their ports. 'I believe,' said Calhoun, 'that the success of a connection of the West is of the last importance to us politically and commercially . . . I do verily believe that Charleston has more advantages in her position for the Western trade, than any city on the Atlantic, but to develop them we ought to look to the Tennessee instead of the Ohio, and much farther to the West than Cincinnati or Lexington.'

This was the secret of Calhoun's advocacy in 1836 and 1837 both of the distribution of the surplus revenue and of the cession of the public lands to the States in which they lay, as an inducement to the West to ally itself with Southern policies; and it is the key to the readiness of Calhoun, even after he lost his nationalism, to promote internal improvements which would foster the southward current of trade on the Mississippi.

Without going into details, I may simply call your attention to the fact that Clay's whole system of internal improvements and tariff was based upon the place of the Mississippi Valley in American life. It was the upper part of the Valley, and especially the Ohio Valley, that furnished the votes which carried the tariffs of 1816, 1824, and 1828. Its interests profoundly influenced the details of those tariffs and its need of internal improvement constituted a basis for sectional bargaining in all the constructive legislation after the War of 1812. New England, the Middle Region, and the South each sought alliance with the growing section beyond the mountains. American legislation bears the enduring evidence of these alliances. Even the National Bank found in this Valley the main sphere of its business. The nation had turned its energies to internal exploitation, and sections contended for the economic and political power derived from connection with the interior.

But already the Mississippi Valley was beginning to stratify, both socially and geographically. As the railroads pushed across the mountains, the tide of New England and New York colonists and German immigrants sought the basin of the Great Lakes and the Upper Mississippi. A distinct zone, industrially and socially connected with New England, was forming. The railroad reinforced the Erie Canal and, as De Bow put it, turned back the tide of the Father of Waters so that its outlet was in New York instead of New Orleans for a large part of the Valley. Below the Northern zone was the border zone of the Upland South, the region of compromise, including both banks of the Ohio and the Missouri and reaching down to the hills on the north of the Gulf Plains. The Cotton Kingdom based on slavery found its center in the fertile soils along the Lower Mississippi and the black prairies of Georgia and Alabama, and was settled largely by planters from the old cotton lands of the Atlantic States. The Mississippi Valley had rejuvenated slavery, had given it an aggressive tone characteristic of Western life.

Thus the Valley found itself in the midst of the slavery struggle at the very time when its own society had lost homogeneity. Let us allow two leaders, one of the South and one of the North, to describe the situation; and, first, let the South speak. Said Hammond, of South Carolina, in a speech in the Senate on March 4, 1858:

I think it not improper that I should attempt to bring the North and South face to face, and see what resources each of us might have in the contingency of separate organizations.

Through the heart of our country runs the great Mississippi, the father of waters, into whose bosom are poured thirty-six thousand miles of tributary streams; and beyond we have the desert prairie wastes to protect us in our rear. Can you hem in such a territory as that? You talk of putting up a wall of fire around eight hundred and fifty thousand miles so situated! How absurd.

But in this territory lies the great valley of the Mississippi, now the real and soon to be the acknowledged seat of the empire of the world. The sway of that valley will be as great as ever the Nile knew in the earlier ages of mankind. We own the most of it. The most valuable part of it belongs to us now; and although those who have settled above us are now opposed to us, another generation will tell a different tale. They are ours by all the laws of nature; slave labor will go to every foot of this great valley where it will be found profitable to use it, and some of those who may not use it are soon to be united with us by such ties as will make us one and inseparable. The iron horse will soon be clattering over the sunny plains of the South to bear the products of its upper tributaries to our Atlantic ports, as it now does through the ice-bound North. There is the great Mississippi, bond of union made by nature herself. She will maintain it forever.

As the Seaboard South had transferred the mantle of leadership to Tennessee and then to the Cotton Kingdom of the Lower Mississippi, so New England and New York resigned their command to the northern half of the Mississippi Valley and the basin of the Great Lakes. Seward, the old-time leader of the Eastern Whigs who had just lost the Republican nomination for the presidency to Lincoln, may rightfully speak for the Northeast. In the fall of 1860, addressing an audience at Madison, Wisconsin, he declared:

The empire established at Washington is of less than a hundred years' formation. It was the empire of thirteen Atlantic states. Still, practically, the mission of that empire is fulfilled. The power that directs it is ready to pass away from those thirteen states, and although held and exercised under the same constitution and national form of government, yet it is now in the very act of being transferred from the thirteen states east of the Alleghany mountains and on the coast of the Atlantic ocean, to the twenty states that lie west of the Alleghanies, and stretch away from their base to the base of the Rocky mountains on the West, and you are the heirs to it. When the next census shall reveal your power, you will be found to be the masters of the United States of America, and through them the dominating political power of the world.

Appealing to the Northwest on the slavery issue Seward declared:

The whole responsibility rests henceforth directly or indirectly on the people of the Northwest . . . There can be no virtue in commercial and manufacturing communities to maintain a democracy, when the democracy themselves do not want a democracy. There is no virtue in Pearl street, in Wall street, in Court street, in Chestnut street, in any other street of great commercial cities, that can save the great democratic government of ours, when you cease to uphold it with your intelligent votes, your strong and mighty hands. You must, therefore, lead us as we heretofore reserved and prepared the way for you. We resign to you the banner of human rights and human liberty, on this continent, and we bid you be firm, bold and onward and then you may hope that we will be able to follow you.

When we survey the course of the slavery struggle in the United States it is clear that the form the question took was due to the Mississippi Valley. The Ordinance of 1787, the Missouri Compromise, the Texas question, the Free Soil agitation, the Compromise of 1850, the Kansas–Nebraska bill, the Dred Scott decision, 'bleeding Kansas' – these are all Mississippi Valley questions, and the mere enumeration makes it plain that it was the Mississippi Valley as an area for expansion which gave the slavery issue its significance in American history. But for this field of expansion, slavery might have fulfilled the expectation of the fathers and gradually died away.

Of the significance of the Mississippi Valley in the Civil War, it is unnecessary that I should speak. Illinois gave to the North its President; Mississippi gave to the South its President. Lincoln and Davis were both born in Kentucky. Grant and Sherman, the northern generals, came from the Mississippi Valley; and both of them believed that when Vicksburg fell the cause of the South was lost, and so it must have been if the Confederacy had been unable, after victories in the East, to regain the Father of Waters; for, as General Sherman said: 'Whatever power holds that river can govern this continent.'

With the close of the war political power passed for many years to the northern half of the Mississippi Valley, as the names of Grant, Hayes, Garfield, Harrison, and McKinley indicate. The population of the Valley grew from about fifteen millions in 1860 to over forty millions in 1900 – over half the total population of the United States. The significance of its industrial growth is not likely to be overestimated or overlooked. On its northern border, from near Minnesota's boundary line, through the Great Lakes to Pittsburgh, on its eastern edge, runs a huge movement of iron from mine to factory. This industry is basal in American life, and it has revolutionized the industry of the world. The United States produces pig-iron and steel in amount equal to her two greatest competitors combined, and the iron ores for this product are chiefly in the Mississippi Valley. It is the chief producer of coal, thereby enabling the United States almost to equal the combined production of Germany and Great Britain; and great oil fields of the nation are in its midst. Its huge crops of wheat and corn and its cattle are the main resources for the United States and are drawn upon by Europe. Its cotton furnishes two-thirds of the world's factory supply. Its railroad system constitutes the greatest transportation network in the world. Again it is seeking industrial consolidation by demanding improvement of its vast water system as a unit. If this design, favored by Roosevelt, shall at some time be accomplished, again the bulk of the commerce of the Valley may flow along the old routes to New Orleans; and to Galveston by the development of southern railroad outlets after the building of the Panama Canal. For the development and exploitation of these and of the transportation and trade interests of the Middle West, Eastern capital has been consolidated into huge corporations, trusts, and combinations. With the influx of capital, and the rise of cities and manufactures, portions of the Mississippi Valley have become assimilated with the East. With the end of the era of free lands the basis of its democratic society is passing away.

The final topic on which I shall briefly comment in

this discussion of the significance of the Mississippi Valley in American history is a corollary of this condition. Has the Mississippi Valley a permanent contribution to make to American society, or is it to be adjusted into a type characteristically Eastern and European? In other words, has the United States itself an original contribution to make to the history of society? This is what it comes to. The most significant fact in the Mississippi Valley is its ideals. Here has been developed, not by revolutionary theory, but by growth among free opportunities, the conception of a vast democracy made up of mobile ascending individuals, conscious of their power and their responsibilities. Can these ideals of individualism and democracy be reconciled and applied to the twentieth century type of civilization?

Other nations have been rich and prosperous and powerful, art-loving and empire-building. No other nation on a vast scale has been controlled by a self-conscious, self-restrained democracy in the interests of progress and freedom, industrial as well as political. It is in the vast and level spaces of the Mississippi Valley, if anywhere, that the forces of social transformation and the modification of its democratic ideals may be arrested.

Beginning with competitive individualism, as well as with belief in equality, the farmers of the Mississippi Valley gradually learned that unrestrained competition and combination meant the triumph of the strongest, the seizure in the interest of a dominant class of the strategic points of the nation's life. They learned that between the ideal of individualism, unrestrained by society, and the ideal of democracy, was an innate conflict; that their very ambitions and forcefulness had endangered their democracy. The significance of the Mississippi Valley in American history has lain partly in the fact that it was a region of revolt. Here have arisen varied, sometimes ill-considered, but always devoted, movements for ameliorating the lot of the common man in the interests of democracy. Out of the Mississippi Valley have come successive and related tidal waves of popular demand for real or imagined legislative safeguards to their rights and their social ideals. The Granger movement, the Greenback movement, the Populist movement, Bryan Democracy, and Roosevelt Republicanism all found their greatest strength in the Mississippi Valley. They were Mississippi Valley ideals in action. Its people were learning by experiment and experience how to grapple with the fundamental problem of creating a just social order that shall sustain the free, progressive, individual in a real democracy. The Mississippi Valley is asking, 'What shall it profit a man if he gain the whole world and lose his own soul?'

The Mississippi Valley has furnished a new social order to America. Its universities have set new types of institutions for social service and for the elevation of the plain people. Its historians should recount its old ambitions, and inventory its ideals, as well as its resources, for the information of the present age, to the end that building on its past, the mighty Valley may have a significance in the life of the nation even more profound than any which I have recounted.

IV

Social Forces in American History (1910)

The transformations through which the United States is passing in our own day are so profound, so far-reaching, that it is hardly an exaggeration to say that we are witnessing the birth of a new nation in America. The revolution in the social and economic structure of this country during the past two decades is comparable to what occurred when independence was declared and the constitution was formed, or to the changes wrought by the era which began half a century ago, the era of Civil War and Reconstruction.

These changes have been long in preparation and are, in part, the result of world-wide forces of reorganization incident to the age of steam production and large-scale industry, and, in part, the result of the closing of the period of the colonization of the West. They have been prophesied, and the course of the movement partly described by students of American development; but after all, it is with a shock that the people of the United States are coming to realize that the fundamental forces which have shaped their society up to the present are disappearing. Twenty years ago, as I have before had occasion to point out, the Superintendent of the Census declared that the frontier line, which its maps had depicted for decade after decade of the westward march of the nation, could no longer be described. To-day we must add that the age of free competition of individuals for the unpossessed resources of the nation is nearing its end. It is taking less than a generation to write the chapter which began with the disappearance of the line of the frontier – the last chapter in the history of the colonization of the United States, the conclusion to the annals of its pioneer democracy.

It is a wonderful chapter, this final rush of American energy upon the remaining wilderness. Even the bare statistics become eloquent of a new era. They no longer derive their significance from the exhibit of vast proportions of the public domain transferred to agriculture, of wildernesses equal to European nations changed decade after decade into the farm area of the United States. It is true there was added to the farms of the nation between 1870 and 1880 a territory equal to that of France, and between 1880 and 1900 a territory equal to the European area of France, Germany, England, and Wales combined. The records of 1910 are not yet available, but whatever they reveal they will not be so full of meaning as the figures which tell of upleaping wealth and organization and concentration of industrial power in the East in the last decade. As the final provinces of the Western empire have been subdued to the purposes of civilization and have yielded their spoils, as the spheres of operation of the great industrial corporations have extended, with the extension of American settlement, production and wealth have increased beyond all precedent.

The total deposits in all national banks have more than trebled in the present decade; the money in circulation has doubled since 1890. The flood of gold makes it difficult to gage the full meaning of the incredible increase in values, for in the decade ending with 1909 over 41,600,000 ounces of gold were mined in the United States alone. Over four million ounces have been produced every year since 1905, whereas between 1880 and 1894 no year showed a production of two million ounces. As a result of this swelling stream of gold and instruments of credit, aided by a variety of other causes, prices have risen until their height has become one of the most marked features and influential factors in American life, producing social readjustments and contributing effectively to party revolutions.

But if we avoid those statistics which require analysis because of the changing standard of value, we still find that the decade occupies an exceptional place in American history. More coal was mined in the United States in the ten years after 1897 than in all the life of the nation before that time. Fifty years ago we mined less than fifteen million long tons of coal. In 1907 we mined nearly 429,000,000. At the present rate it is estimated that the supply of coal would be exhausted at a date no farther in the future than the formation of the constitution is in the past. Iron and coal are the measures of industrial power. The nation has produced three times as much iron ore in the past two decades as in all its previous history; the production of the past ten years was more than double that of the prior decade. Pig-iron production is admitted to be an excellent barometer of manufacture and of transportation. Never until 1898 had this reached an annual total of ten million long tons. But in the five years beginning with 1904 it averaged over twice that. By 1907 the United States had surpassed Great Britain, Germany, and France combined in the production of pig-iron and steel together, and in the same decade a single great corporation has established its domination over the iron mines and steel manufacture of the United States. It is more than a mere accident that the United States Steel Corporation with its stocks and bonds aggregating $1,400,000,000 was organized at the beginning of the present decade. The former wilderness about Lake Superior has, principally in the past two decades, established its position as overwhelmingly the preponderant source of iron ore, present and prospective, in the United States – a treasury from which Pittsburgh has drawn wealth and extended its unparalleled industrial empire in these years. The tremendous energies thus liberated at this center of industrial power in the United States revolutionized methods of manufacture in general, and in many indirect ways profoundly influenced the life of the nation.

Railroad statistics also exhibit unprecedented development, the formation of a new industrial society. The number of passengers carried one mile more than doubled between 1890 and 1908; freight carried one mile has nearly trebled in the same period and has doubled in the past decade. Agricultural products tell a different story. The corn crop has only risen from about two billion bushels in 1891 to two and seven-tenths billions in 1909; wheat from six hundred and eleven million bushels in 1891 to only seven hundred and thirty-seven million in 1909; and cotton from about nine million bales in 1891 to ten and three-tenths million bales in 1909. Population has increased in the United States proper from about sixty-two and one-half millions in 1890 to seventy-five and one-half millions in 1900 and to over ninety millions in 1910.

It is clear from these statistics that the ratio of the nation's increased production of immediate wealth by the enormously increased exploitation of its remaining natural resources vastly exceeds the ratio of increase of population and still more strikingly exceeds the ratio of increase of agricultural products. Already population is pressing upon the food supply while capital consolidates in billion-dollar organizations. The 'Triumphant Democracy' whose achievements the iron-master celebrated has reached a stature even more imposing than he could have foreseen; but still less did he perceive the changes in democracy itself and the conditions of its life which have accompanied this material growth.

Having colonized the Far West, having mastered its internal resources, the nation turned at the conclusion of the nineteenth and the beginning of the twentieth century to deal with the Far East, to engage in the world-politics of the Pacific Ocean. Having continued its historic expansion into the lands of the old Spanish empire by the successful outcome of the recent war, the United States became the mistress of the Philippines at the same time that it came into possession of the Hawaiian Islands, and the controlling influence in the Gulf of Mexico. It provided early in the present decade for connecting its Atlantic and Pacific coasts by the Isthmian Canal, and became an imperial republic with dependencies and protectorates – admittedly a new world-power, with a potential voice in the problems of Europe, Asia, and Africa.

This extension of power, this undertaking of grave responsibilities in new fields, this entry into the sisterhood of world-states, was no isolated event. It was, indeed, in some respects the logical outcome of the nation's march to the Pacific, the sequence to the era in which it was engaged in occupying the free lands and exploiting the resources of the West. When it had achieved this position among the nations of the earth, the United States found itself confronted, also, with the need of constitutional readjustment, arising from the relations of federal government and territorial acquisitions. It was obliged to reconsider questions of the rights of man and traditional American ideals of liberty and democracy, in view of the task of government of other races politically inexperienced and undeveloped.

If we turn to consider the effect upon American society and domestic policy in these two decades of transition we are met with palpable evidences of the invasion of the old pioneer democratic order. Obvious among them is the effect of unprecedented immigration to supply the mobile army of cheap labor for the centers of industrial life. In the past ten years, beginning with 1900, over eight million immigrants have arrived. The newcomers of the eight years since 1900 would, according to a writer in 1908, 'repopulate all the five older New England States as they stand to-day; or, if properly disseminated over the newer parts of the country they would serve to populate no less than nineteen states of the Union as they stand.' In 1907 'there were one and one-quarter million arrivals. This number would entirely populate both New Hampshire and Maine, two of our oldest States.' 'The arrivals of this one year would found a State with more inhabitants than any one of twenty-one of our other existing commonwealths which could be named.' Not only has the addition to the population from Europe been thus extraordinary, it has come in increasing measure from southern and eastern Europe. For the year 1907, Professor Ripley, whom I am quoting, has redistributed the incomers on the basis of physical type and finds that one-quarter of them were of the Mediterranean race, one-quarter of the Slavic race, one-eighth Jewish, and only one-sixth of the Alpine, and one-sixth of the Teutonic. In 1882 Germans had come to the amount of 250,000; in 1907 they were replaced by 330,000 South Italians. Thus it is evident that the ethnic elements of the United States have undergone startling changes; and instead of spreading over the nation these immigrants have concentrated especially in the cities and great industrial centers in the past decade. The composition of the labor class and its relation to wages and to the native American employer have been deeply influenced thereby; the sympathy of the employers with labor has been unfavorably affected by the pressure of great numbers of immigrants of alien nationality and of lower standards of life.

The familiar facts of the massing of population in the cities and the contemporaneous increase of urban power, and of the massing of capital and production in fewer and vastly greater industrial units, especially attest the revolution. 'It is a proposition too plain to require eluci- dation,' wrote Richard Rush, Secretary of the Treasury, in his report of 1827, 'that the creation of capital is retarded rather than accelerated by the diffusion of a thin population over a great surface of soil.' Thirty years before Rush wrote these words Albert Gallatin declared in Congress that 'if the cause of the happiness of this country were examined into, it would be found to arise as much from the great plenty of land in proportion to the inhabitants which their citizens enjoyed as from the wisdom of their political institutions.' Possibly both of these Pennsylvania financiers were right under the con- ditions of the time; but it is at least significant that capital and labor entered upon a new era as the end of the free lands approached. A contemporary of Gallatin in Congress had replied to the argument that cheap lands would depopulate the Atlantic coast by saying that if a law were framed to prevent ready access to western lands it would be tantamount to saying that there is some class which must remain 'and by law be obliged to serve the others for such wages as they pleased to give.' The passage of the arable public domain into private possession has raised this question in a new form and has brought forth new answers. This is peculiarly the era when competitive individualism in the midst of vast unappropriated opportunities changed into the mon- opoly of the fundamental industrial processes by huge aggregations of capital as the free lands disappeared. All the tendencies of the large-scale production of the twentieth century, all the trend to the massing of capital in large combinations, all of the energies of the age of steam, found in America exceptional freedom of action and were offered regions of activity equal to the states of all Western Europe. Here they reached their highest development.

The decade following 1897 is marked by the work of Mr Harriman and his rivals in building up the various railroads into a few great groups, a process that had gone so far that before his death Mr Harriman was ambitious to concentrate them all under his single control. High finance under the leadership of Mr Morgan steadily achieved the consolidation of the greater industries into trusts or combinations and effected a community of interests between them and a few dominant banking organizations, with allied insurance companies and trust companies. In New York City have been centered, as never before, the banking reserves of the nation, and here, by the financial management of capital and speculative promotion, there has grown up a unified control over the nation's industrial life. Colossal private fortunes have arisen. No longer is the per capita wealth of the nation a real index to the prosperity of the average man. Labor on the other hand has shown an increasing self-consciousness, is combining and increasing its demands. In a word, the old pioneer individualism is disappearing, while the forces of social combination are manifesting themselves as never before. The self-made man has become, in popular speech, the coal baron, the steel king, the oil king, the cattle king, the railroad magnate, the master of high finance, the monarch of trusts. The world has never before seen such huge fortunes exercising combined control over the economic life of a people, and such luxury as has come out of the individualistic pioneer democracy of America in the course of competitive evolution.

At the same time the masters of industry, who control interests which represent billions of dollars, do not admit that they have broken with pioneer ideals. They regard themselves as pioneers under changed conditions, carrying on the old work of developing the natural resources of the nation, compelled by the constructive fever in their veins, even in ill-health and old age and after the accumulation of wealth beyond their power to enjoy, to seek new avenues of action and of power, to chop new clearings, to find new trails, to expand the horizon of the nation's activity, and to extend the scope of their dominion. 'This country,' said the late Mr Harriman in an interview a few years ago, 'has been developed by a wonderful people, flush with enthusiasm, imagination and speculative bent ... They have been magnificent pioneers. They saw into the future and adapted their work to the possibilities ... Stifle that enthusiasm, deaden that imagination and prohibit that speculation by restrictive and cramping conservative law, and you tend to produce a moribund and conservative people and country.' This is an appeal to the historic ideals of Americans who viewed the republic as the guardian of individual freedom to compete for the control of the natural resources of the nation.

On the other hand, we have the voice of the insurgent West, recently given utterance in the New Nationalism of ex-President Roosevelt, demanding increase of federal authority to curb the special interests, the powerful industrial organizations, and the monopolies, for the sake of the conservation of our natural resources and the preservation of American democracy.

The past decade has witnessed an extraordinary federal activity in limiting individual and corporate freedom for the benefit of society. To that decade belong the conservation congresses and the effective organization of the Forest Service, and the Reclamation Service. Taken together these developments alone would mark a new era, for over three hundred million acres are, as a result of this policy, reserved from entry and sale, an area more than equal to that of all the states which established the constitution, if we exclude their western claims; and these reserved lands are held for a more beneficial use of their forests, minerals, arid tracts, and water rights, by the nation as a whole. Another example is the extension of the activity of the Department of Agriculture, which seeks the remotest regions of the earth for crops suitable to the areas reclaimed by the government, maps and analyzes the soils, fosters the improvement of seeds and animals, tells the farmer when and how and what to plant, and makes war upon diseases of plants and animals and insect pests. The recent legislation for pure food and meat inspection, and the whole mass of regulative law under the Interstate Commerce clause of the constitution, further illustrates the same tendency.

Two ideals were fundamental in traditional American thought, ideals that developed in the pioneer era. One was that of individual freedom to compete unrestrictedly for the resources of a continent – the squatter ideal. To the pioneer government was an evil. The other was the ideal of a democracy – 'government of the people, by the people and for the people.' The operation of these ideals took place contemporaneously with the passing into private possession of the free public domain and the natural resources of the United States. But American democracy was based on an abundance of free lands; these were the very conditions that shaped its growth and its fundamental traits. Thus time has revealed that these two ideals of pioneer democracy had elements of mutual hostility and contained the seeds of its dissolution. The present finds itself engaged in the task of readjusting its old ideals to new conditions and is turning increasingly to government to preserve its traditional democracy. It is not surprising that socialism shows noteworthy gains as elections continue; that parties are forming on new lines; that the demand for primary elections, for popular choice of senators, initiative, referendum, and recall, is spreading, and that the regions once the center of pioneer democracy exhibit these tendencies in the most marked degree. They are efforts to find substitutes for that former safeguard of democracy, the disappearing free lands. They are the sequence to the extinction of the frontier.

It is necessary next to notice that in the midst of all this national energy, and contemporaneous with the tendency to turn to the national government for protection to democracy, there is clear evidence of the persistence and the development of sectionalism. Whether we observe the grouping of votes in Congress and in general elections, or the organization and utterances of business leaders, or the association of scholars, churches, or other representatives of the things of the spirit, we find that American life is not only increasing in its national intensity but that it is integrating by sections. In part this is due to the factor of great spaces which make sectional rather than national organization the line of least resistance; but, in part, it is also the expression of the separate economic, political, and social interests and the separate spiritual life of the various geographic provinces or sections. The votes on the tariff, and in general the location of the strongholds of the Progressive Republican movement, illustrate this fact. The difficulty of a national adjustment of railway rates to the diverse interests of different sections is another example. Without attempting to enter upon a more extensive discussion of sectionalism, I desire simply to point out that there are evidences that now, as formerly, the separate geographical interests have their leaders and spokesmen, that much Congressional legislation is determined by the contests, triumphs, or compromises between the rival sections, and that the real federal relations of the United States are shaped by the interplay of sectional with national forces rather than by the relation of State and Nation. As time goes on and the nation adjusts itself more durably to the conditions of the differing geographic sections which make it up, they are coming to a new self-consciousness and a revived self-assertion. Our national character is a composite of these sections.

Obviously in attempting to indicate even a portion of the significant features of our recent history we have been obliged to take note of a complex of forces. The times are so close at hand that the relations between events and tendencies force themselves upon our attention. We have had to deal with the connections of geography, industrial growth, politics, and government. With these we must take into consideration the changing social composition, the inherited beliefs and habitual attitude of the masses of the people, the psychology of the nation and of the separate sections, as well as of the leaders. We must see how these leaders are shaped partly by their time and section, and how they are in part original, creative, by virtue of their own genius and initiative. We cannot neglect the moral tendencies and the ideals. All are related parts of the same subject and can no more be properly understood in isolation than the movement as a whole can be understood by neglecting some of these important factors, or by the use of a single method of investigation. Whatever be the truth regarding European history, American history is chiefly concerned with social forces, shaping and reshaping under the conditions of a nation changing as it adjusts to its environment. And this environment progressively reveals new aspects of itself, exerts new influences, and calls out new social organs and functions.

I have undertaken this rapid survey of recent history for two purposes. First, because it has seemed fitting to emphasize the significance of American development since the passing of the frontier, and, second, because in the observation of present conditions we may find assistance in our study of the past.

It is a familiar doctrine that each age studies its history

anew and with interests determined by the spirit of the time. Each age finds it necessary to reconsider at least some portion of the past, from points of view furnished by new conditions which reveal the influence and significance of forces not adequately known by the historians of the previous generation. Unquestionably each investigator and writer is influenced by the times in which he lives and while this fact exposes the historian to a bias, at the same time it affords him new instruments and new insight for dealing with his subject.

If recent history, then, gives new meaning to past events, if it has to deal with the rise into a commanding position of forces, the origin and growth of which may have been inadequately described or even overlooked by historians of the previous generation, it is important to study the present and the recent past, not only for themselves but also as the source of new hypotheses, new lines of inquiry, new criteria of the perspective of the remoter past. And, moreover, a just public opinion and a statesmanlike treatment of present problems demand that they be seen in their historical relations in order that history may hold the lamp for conservative reform.

Seen from the vantage-ground of present developments what new light falls upon past events! When we consider what the Mississippi Valley has come to be in American life, and when we consider what it is yet to be, the young Washington, crossing the snows of the wilderness to summon the French to evacuate the portals of the great valley, becomes the herald of an empire. When we recall the huge industrial power that has centered at Pittsburgh, Braddock's advance to the forks of the Ohio takes on new meaning. Even in defeat, he opened a road to what is now the center of the world's industrial energy. The modifications which England proposed in 1794 to John Jay in the northwestern boundary of the United States from the Lake of the Woods to the Mississippi, seemed to him, doubtless, significant chiefly as a matter of principle and as a question of the retention or loss of beaver grounds. The historians hardly notice the proposals. But they involved, in fact, the ownership of the richest and most extensive deposits of iron ore in America, the all-important source of a fundamental industry of the United States, the occasion for the rise of some of the most influential forces of our time.

What continuity and meaning are furnished by the outcome in present times of the movements of minor political parties and reform agitations! To the historian they have often seemed to be mere curious side eddies, vexatious distractions to the course of his literary craft as it navigated the stream of historical tendency. And yet, by the revelation of the present, what seemed to be side eddies have not seldom proven to be the concealed entrances to the main current, and the course which seemed the central one has led to blind channels and stagnant waters, important in their day, but cut off like ox-bow lakes from the mighty river of historical progress by the mere permanent and compelling forces of the neglected currents.

We may trace the contest between the capitalist and the democratic pioneer from the earliest colonial days. It is influential in colonial parties. It is seen in the vehement protests of Kentucky frontiersmen in petition after petition to the Congress of the Confederation against the 'nabobs' and men of wealth who took out titles to the pioneers' farms while they themselves were too busy defending those farms from the Indians to perfect their claims. It is seen in the attitude of the Ohio Valley in its backwoods days before the rise of the Whig party, as when in 1811 Henry Clay denounced the Bank of the United States as a corporation which throve on special privileges – 'a special association of favored individuals taken from the mass of society, and invested with exemptions and surrounded by immunities and privileges.' Benton voiced the same contest twenty years later when he denounced the bank as

a company of private individuals, many of them foreigners, and the mass of them residing in a remote and narrow corner of the Union, unconnected by any sympathy with the fertile regions of the Great Valley in which the natural power of this Union, the power of numbers, will be found to reside long before the renewed term of the second charter would expire.

'And where,' he asked, 'would all this power and money center? In the great cities of the Northeast, which have been for forty years and that by force of federal legislation, the lion's den of Southern and Western money – that den into which all the tracks point inward; from which the returning track of a solitary dollar has never yet been seen.' Declaring, in words that have a very modern sound, that the bank tended to multiply nabobs and paupers, and that 'a great moneyed power is favorable to great capitalists, for it is the principle of capital to favor capital,' he appealed to the fact of the country's extent and its sectional divergences against the nationalizing of capital.

What a condition for a confederacy of states! What grounds for alarm and terrible apprehension when in a confederacy of such vast extent, so many rival commercial cities, so much sectional jealousy, such violent political parties, such fierce contests for power, there should be but one moneyed tribunal before which all the rival and contending elements must appear.

Even more vehement were the words of Jackson in 1837. 'It is now plain,' he wrote, 'that the war is to be carried on by the monied aristocracy of the few against the democracy of numbers; the [prosperous] to make the honest laborers hewers of wood and drawers of water through the credit and paper system.'

Van Buren's administration is usually passed hastily over with hardly more than mention of his Independent Treasury plan, and with particular consideration of the slavery discussion. But some of the most important movements in American social and political history began in these years of Jackson and Van Buren. Read the demands of the obscure labor papers and the reports of labor's open-air meetings anew, and you will find in the utterances of so-called labor visionaries and the Locofoco champions of 'equal rights for all and special privileges for none,' like Evans and Jacques, Byrdsall and Leggett, the finger points to the currents that now make the main channel of our history; you will find in them some of the important planks of the platforms of the triumphant parties of our own day. As Professor Commons has shown by his papers and the documents which he has published on labor history, an idealistic but widespread and influential humanitarian movement, strikingly similar to that of the present, arose in the years between 1830 and 1850, dealing with social forces in American life, animated by a desire to apply the public lands to social amelioration, eager to find new forms of democratic development. But the flood of the slavery struggle swept all of these movements into its mighty inundation for the time. After the war, other influences delayed the revival of the movement. The railroads opened the wide prairies after 1850 and made it easy to reach them; and decade after decade new sections were reduced to the purposes of civilization and to the advantages of the common man as well as the promotion of great individual fortunes. The nation centered its interests in the development of the West. It is only in our own day that this humanitarian democratic wave has reached the level of those earlier years. But in the meantime there are clear evidences of the persistence of the forces, even though under strange guise. Read the platforms of the Greenback-Labor, the Granger, and the Populist parties, and you will find in those platforms, discredited and reprobated by the major parties of the time, the basic proposals of the Democratic party after its revolution under the leadership of Mr Bryan, and of the Republican party after its revolution by Mr Roosevelt. The Insurgent movement is so clearly related to the areas and elements that gave strength to this progressive assertion of old democratic ideals with new weapons, that it must be regarded as the organized refusal of these persistent tendencies to be checked by the advocates of more moderate measures.

I have dealt with these fragments of party history, not, of course, with the purpose of expressing any present judgment upon them, but to emphasize and give concreteness to the fact that there is disclosed by present events a new significance to these contests of radical democracy and conservative interests; that they are rather a continuing expression of deep-seated forces than fragmentary and sporadic curios for the historical museum.

If we should survey the history of our lands from a similar point of view, considering the relations of legislation and administration of the public domain to the structure of American democracy, it would yield a return far beyond that offered by the formal treatment of the subject in most of our histories. We should find in the squatter doctrines and practices, the seizure of the best soils, the taking of public timber on the theory of a right to it by the labor expended on it, fruitful material for understanding the atmosphere and ideals under which the great corporations developed the West. Men like Senator Benton and Delegate Sibley in successive generations defended the trespasses of the pioneer and the lumberman upon the public forest lands, and denounced the paternal government that 'harassed' these men, who were engaged in what we should call stealing government timber. It is evident that at some time between the middle of the nineteenth century and the present time, when we impose jail sentences upon Congressmen caught in such violations of the land laws, a change came over the American conscience and the civic ideals were modified. That our great industrial enterprises developed in the midst of these changing ideals is important to recall when we write the history of their activity.

We should find also that we cannot understand the land question without seeing its relations to the struggle of sections and classes bidding against each other and finding in the public domain a most important topic of political bargaining. We should find, too, that the settlement of unlike geographic areas in the course of the nation's progress resulted in changes in the effect of the land laws; that a system intended for the humid prairies was ill-adjusted to the grazing lands and coal fields and to the forests in the days of large-scale exploitation by corporations commanding great capital. Thus changing geographic factors as well as the changing character of the forces which occupied the public domain must be considered, if we would understand the bearing of legislation and policy in this field. It is fortunate that suggestive studies of democracy and the land policy have already begun to appear.

The whole subject of American agriculture viewed in relation to the economic, political, and social life of the nation has important contributions to make. If, for example, we study the maps showing the transition of the wheat belt from the East to the West, as the virgin soils were conquered and made new bases for destructive competition with the older wheat States, we shall see how deeply they affected not only land values, railroad building, the movement of population, and the supply of cheap food, but also how the regions once devoted to single cropping of wheat were forced to turn to varied and intensive agriculture and to diversified industry, and we shall see also how these transformations affected party politics and even the ideals of the Americans of the regions thus changed. We shall find in the over-production of wheat in the provinces thus rapidly colonized, and in the over-production of silver in the mountain provinces which were contemporaneously exploited, important explanations of the peculiar form which American politics took in the period when Mr Bryan mastered the Democratic party, just as we shall find in the opening of the new gold fields in the years immediately following, and in the passing of the era of almost free virgin wheat soils, explanations of the more recent period when high prices are giving new energy and aggressiveness to the demands of the new American industrial democracy.

Enough has been said, it may be assumed, to make clear the point which I am trying to elucidate, namely that a comprehension of the United States of to-day, an understanding of the rise and progress of the forces which have made it what it is, demands that we should rework our history from the new points of view afforded by the present. If this is done, it will be seen, for example, that the progress of the struggle between North and South over slavery and the freed negro, which held the principal place in American interest in the two decades after 1850, was, after all, only one of the interests in the time. The pages of the Congressional debates, the contemporary newspapers, the public documents of those twenty years, remain a rich mine for those who will seek therein the sources of movements dominant in the present day.

The final consideration to which I ask your attention in this discussion of social forces in American life, is with reference to the mode of investigating them and the bearing of these investigations upon the relations and the goal of history. It has become a precedent, fairly well established by the distinguished scholars who have held the office which I am about to lay down, to state a position with reference to the relations of history and its sister-studies, and even to raise the question of the attitude of the historian toward the laws of thermodynamics and to seek to find the key of historical development or of historical degradation. It is not given to all to bend the bow of Ulysses. I shall attempt a lesser task.

We may take some lessons from the scientist. He has enriched knowledge especially in recent years by attacking the no-man's lands left unexplored by the too sharp delimitation of spheres of activity. These new conquests have been especially achieved by the combination of old sciences. Physical chemistry, electro-chemistry, geo-physics, astro-physics, and a variety of other scientific unions have led to audacious hypotheses, veritable flashes of vision, which open new regions of activity for a generation of investigators. Moreover they have promoted such investigations by furnishing new instruments of research. Now in some respects there is an analogy between geology and history. The new geologist aims to describe the inorganic earth dynamically in terms of natural law, using chemistry, physics, mathematics, and even botany and zoology so far as they relate to paleontology. But he does not insist that the relative importance of physical or chemical factors shall be determined before he applies the methods and data of these sciences to his problem. Indeed, he has learned that a geological area is too complex a thing to be reduced to a single explanation. He has abandoned the single hypothesis for the multiple hypothesis. He creates a whole family of possible explanations of a given problem and thus avoids the warping influence of partiality for a simple theory.

Have we not here an illustration of what is possible and necessary for the historian? Is it not well, before attempting to decide whether history requires an economic interpretation, or a psychological, or any other ultimate interpretation, to recognize that the factors in human society are varied and complex; that the political historian handling his subject in isolation is certain to miss fundamental facts and relations in his treatment of a given age or nation; that the economic historian is exposed to the same danger; and so of all of the other special historians?

Those who insist that history is simply the effort to tell the thing exactly as it was, to state the facts, are confronted with the difficulty that the fact which they would represent is not planted on the solid ground of fixed conditions; it is in the midst and is itself a part of the changing currents, the complex and interacting influences of the time, deriving its significance as a fact from its relations to the deeper-seated movements of the age, movements so gradual that often only the passing years can reveal the truth about the fact and its right to a place on the historian's page.

The economic historian is in danger of making his analysis and his statement of a law on the basis of present conditions and then passing to history for justificatory appendixes to his conclusions. An American economist of high rank has recently expressed his conception of 'the full relation of economic theory, statistics, and history' in these words:

A principle is formulated by *a priori* reasoning concerning facts of common experience; it is then tested by statistics and promoted to the rank of a known and acknowledged truth; illustrations of its action are then found in narrative history and, on the other hand, the economic law becomes the interpreter of records that would otherwise be confusing and comparatively valueless; the law itself derives its final confirmation from the illustrations of its working which the records afford; but what is at least of equal importance is the parallel fact that the law affords the decisive test of the correctness of those assertions concerning the causes and the effects of past events which it is second nature to make and which historians almost invariably do make in connection with their narrations.

There is much in this statement by which the historian may profit, but he may doubt also whether the past should serve merely as the 'illustration' by which to confirm the law deduced from common experience by *a priori* reasoning tested by statistics. In fact the pathway of history is strewn with the wrecks of the 'known and acknowledged truths' of economic law, due not only to defective analysis and imperfect statistics, but also to the lack of critical historical methods, of insufficient historical-mindedness on the part of the economist, to failure to give due attention to the relativity and transiency of the conditions from which his laws were deduced.

But the point on which I would lay stress is this. The economist, the political scientist, the psychologist, the sociologist, the geographer, the student of literature; of art, of religion – all the allied laborers in the study of society – have contributions to make to the equipment of the historian. These contributions are partly of material, partly of tools, partly of new points of view, new hypotheses, new suggestions of relations, causes, and emphasis. Each of these special students is in some danger of bias by his particular point of view, by his exposure to see simply the thing in which he is primarily interested, and also by his effort to deduce the universal laws of his separate science. The historian, on the other hand, is exposed to the danger of dealing with the complex and interacting social forces of a period or of a country, from some single point of view to which his special training or interest inclines him. If the truth is to be made known, the historian must so far familiarize himself with the work, and equip himself with the training of his sister-subjects that he can at least avail himself of their results and in some reasonable degree master the essential tools of their trade. And the followers of the sister-studies must likewise familiarize themselves and their students with the work and the methods of the historians, and cooperate in the difficult task.

It is necessary that the American historian shall aim at this equipment, not so much that he may possess the key to history or satisfy himself in regard to its ultimate laws. At present a different duty is before him. He must see in American society with its vast spaces, its sections equal to European nations, its geographic influences, its brief period of development, its variety of nationalities and races, its extraordinary industrial growth under the conditions of freedom, its institutions, culture, ideals, social psychology, and even its religions forming and changing almost under his eyes, one of the richest fields ever offered for the preliminary recognition and study of the forces that operate and interplay in the making of society.